The

GREYSTON BAKERY COOKBOOK

The
GREYSTON BAKERY
COOKBOOK

MORE THAN 80 RECIPES TO INSPIRE
THE WAY YOU COOK AND LIVE

SARA KATE GILLINGHAM-RYAN

Rodale books may be purchased for business
or promotional use or for special sales.
For information, please write to:
Special Markets Department, Rodale Inc.,
733 Third Avenue, New York, NY 10017

Printed in the United States of America
Rodale Inc. makes every effort to use acid-free ∞, recycled paper ♲.

Photo credits can be found on page 187.
Interior design by Cindy Goldstein, Eric Baker Design
Cover design by Cindy Goldstein, Eric Baker Design

Library of Congress Cataloging-in-Publication Data
Gillingham-Ryan, Sara Kate.
    The Greyston Bakery cookbook : 75 recipes to inspire the way you cook and live / Sara Kate
Gillingham-Ryan.
        p.   cm.
    Includes bibliographical references and index.
    ISBN-13 978-1-59486-621-0   hardcover
    ISBN-10 1-59486-621-X   hardcover
    1. Baking.   2. Greyston Bakery.   I. Title.
TX763.G4375 2007
641.7'1—dc22   2006100806

DISTRIBUTED TO THE TRADE BY HOLTZBRINCK PUBLISHERS

2   4   6   8   10   9   7   5   3   1   hardcover

We inspire and enable people to improve their lives and the world around them
For more of our products visit **rodalestore.com** or call 800-848-4735

*This book is dedicated
to the Greyston family. May your lives
continue to be nourished and sweetened
by serving and being served
at Greyston.*

CONTENTS

ACKNOWLEDGMENTS

My life is rich because of the experience I had working at the Greyston Foundation and having the opportunity both to serve the people of Yonkers and enjoy great cookies, cakes, and tarts along the way. So when I received a phone call a few years ago from Chuck Lief, my old boss at Greyston, asking me if I might be interested in writing a cookbook about Greyston, I leaped at the chance.

Chuck Lief has been a mentor and a friend to me for 10 years, staying in touch after we both left Greyston. To be able to turn to Chuck, whether for advice on a business matter or help with a recipe, is truly a gift. He approaches everything he does with an open heart, even if it is often cloaked in a business suit, and he's a great cook. We should all be so lucky to know someone like Chuck.

Without Julius Walls Jr., the Greyston Bakery's dedicated and passionate leader, the bakery would not be what it is today. He was a supporter of the book from day one, and I thank him for the trust he had in me to make a book that represented the bakery as the beautiful place it is, both in its desserts and its mission.

Also at the bakery, Lisa Salzman was instrumental in getting me old copies of recipes, arranging interviews, and always making me feel welcome when I spent time at the bakery, working the lines in my hairnet and special bakery lab coat. Nothing feels more official than a uniform, and yet it was the spirit in those chocolate-scented halls that made me always feel part of the family.

At the Greyston Foundation, a number of people helped piece together the Greyston story with remembrances and photographs. Thank you to Steve Brown, Lydia Randolph, Shelley Weintraub, and Sarah Brown.

Rozanne Gold has been a dedicated friend of Greyston from the early days, long before I arrived. She remains as dedicated today as she was the day she joined the board of the bakery. We became fast friends as she offered her help with the book. She contributed recipes and carte blanche to call anytime. I did, and I will continue to seek her out, not just for her expertise, but to enjoy her company.

Margot Schupf at Rodale took the time and had the patience to help me turn an idea into a book. I thank her for her confidence in me as a vehicle for getting the Greyston story told.

Amy Super was an ever-upbeat editor who made the whole project seem doable. Even as I was developing recipes, 8-months pregnant, in the middle of a heat wave, Amy always lent her support in the calm, gentle way that helped me push through.

Rodney North at Equal Exchange was generous with chocolate and with helping me understand the importance of supporting the Fair Trade movement. Jamie Johnson at Organic Valley was generous with dairy products and with helping me understand the importance of supporting family farms. I thank them both for their kindness.

The book is as beautiful as it is because of the talents of Carol Angstadt at Rodale and Eric Baker Design, who brought together all the elements and made a package that exceeded my high hopes. John Kelly took the photographs of the desserts. He is not only my favorite food photographer, but a kind and caring person, so there is no one else I would have considered for the project. Asking Karen Gillingham to style the food was another no-brainer, partly because she is my mother and partly because she is so good at what she does. She knew the recipes intimately because she also helped test so many of them.

I was pregnant with my first child during the months the book was written, so I thank my husband, Maxwell, for helping me arrange our lives so that I could take on this project. I thank our community of friends who withstood night after night of dessert trolleys and enforced panel discussions on the flavors and textures of the latest confection.

Finally, there are many people who work at the bakery, live in Greyston housing, or participate in Greyston's programs who shared their stories with me, and for this I thank them and wish them sweetness and nourishment in everything they do.

PREFACE

✳ ✳ ✳

Twenty years ago, Ben and Jerry's began a great journey with the Greyston Bakery. Today, the partnership remains strong and important to both companies.

In 1987, Greyston was full of promise. Its founder, Bernie Glassman, had the audacity to think that a small group of dedicated activists, operating a bakery that hired the homeless and the unemployed, could help transform a low-income community in Yonkers, New York. At the same time, Ben and Jerry's was producing terrific ice cream and was committed to supporting farmers, respecting our employees, and caring about the environment.

Ben and Bernie met at a conference in Colorado, and we found out that the bakers of Greyston were game to stretch and bake brownies for our ice cream. The idea that our purchasing power might help the Greyston social enterprise meet its mission was really exciting to us. Brownies and ice cream—helping to empower a community—was a match made in heaven.

Since that first batch of brownies was baked and shipped from inner-city Yonkers to our Green Mountains in Vermont, more than 25 million pounds of little fellow travelers have made the same trip, finding their way into many best-selling Ben and Jerry's products and supporting the hundreds of bakers whose own journeys took them to Greyston over the years. Like any business relationship, ours has not always been easy. But the connection was always about more than business. Ben and Jerry's employees care about Greyston and have been generous with their time and knowledge. The Greyston crew inspires us. They are proud of the bakery and of the housing, child care, youth programs, and AIDS health care programs that the bakery revenues help support. Also, they are not embarrassed that they needed a helping hand and stand ready to offer the same help to their neighbors.

We know that each recipe you bake will make you happy. We hope that the Greyston story will inspire each of you to find ways to make a difference. Our message is simple: Eat a treat and change the world.

—BEN COHEN & JERRY GREENFIELD

INTRODUCTION

* * *

This is a book about the Greyston Bakery in Yonkers, New York, where cooking for others and cooking for the self, both literally and metaphorically, are practiced daily. I invite you to taste the strong relationship between food and compassion, as well as the role of sweetness in our lives.

I came to the Greyston family fresh from college in 1997 to work for the Greyston Foundation, the nonprofit organization that was borne from the bakery. I spent 4 years working in different capacities at Greyston before moving on to other nonprofit organizations and eventually finding a home in the food business as a writer. The ethics I absorbed during my time at Greyston inform my work. And when the opportunity arose to write a cookbook based on the Greyston specialties, it was a tantalizing offer that I couldn't resist.

It is impossible to share the Greyston Bakery's recipes without also first telling the story of the bakery and the foundation and how the two work together. Be prepared for inspiration in the kitchen and also in your heart.

❦

The Greyston Bakery opened its doors in 1982 in Riverdale, an affluent section of the Bronx just north of Manhattan. Bernie Glassman, a Brooklyn-born applied mathematician and Zen Buddhism teacher, lived with his students in a nearby house. This house, called the Greyston Mansion, sat on the Hudson River and had been originally built as a summer home for the Dodge family. With Glassman as its leader, the Zen Community of New York (ZCNY) opened the bakery, then just a small café, as a way to employ students and provide a place for them to practice mindfulness, hard work, and service, three of the basic tenets of Zen Buddhism.

This model was not unknown in the American Buddhist community. The Tassajara Bakery and the Greens Restaurant in San Francisco are just two examples of other food-related businesses that were opened with the purpose of sustaining the spiritual community. While Glassman's café successfully supported his students, he longed to engage more in community development, to work with the homeless and the chronically unemployed. This desire stemmed from the belief in a central tenet in Buddhism called *right livelihood:* to choose a vocation that brings benefit to oneself and to others.

Glassman's opportunity came just a few years later when the mayor of Yonkers invited the ZCNY to move their business a few miles north. Yonkers, a city upriver from Riverdale, had the highest per capita homeless population in the nation at the time. Without hesitation, the Greyston Mansion was sold, the café was closed, and the group moved to one of the most blighted neighborhoods of Yonkers. There, in an abandoned lasagna factory, the Greyston Bakery was born.

Glassman knew that he needed powerful commitments to make this project work. He asked six people to give a few years of their lives to the bakery. None of the six, nor Glassman, was a baker. None were businesspeople. Starting capital was very limited. The six members began by traveling to the Tassajara Bakery in San Francisco for training and inspiration.

The kitchen in the Monastery of the Blessed Sacrament

In the beginning, the bakery was entirely staffed by members of the ZCNY. The day would start at 5 in the morning with 2 hours of meditation in the third-floor meditation hall in the renovated factory. By 7, baking would start on the first floor of the factory. After several years—as a main ingredient of Greyston's social action practice—the community began to hire people from the neighborhood, many of whom had been unable to hold down stable jobs or lead stable lives because they lacked education or spent time in prison or rehabilitation programs.

With the leadership of Charles Lief, then-president of the Greyston Foundation, and Julius Walls Jr., president and CEO of the Greyston Bakery, the bakery moved to its current home. The bakery is now located in a dazzling 23,000-square-foot facility designed by architect and artist Maya Lin, famous for designing the Vietnam Veterans' Memorial in Washington, DC, and architects Cybul & Cybul. The American Institute of Architects has featured the building on its Web site (www.aiatopten.org/hpb/overview.cfm?ProjectID=299), awarding it a Green Project Award.

Today, the Greyston Bakery is a $6 million-a-year business that employs about 60 local Yonkers residents, many of whom struggle with socioeconomic challenges. The bakery makes baked-from-scratch desserts that are sold on-site, on its Web site (www.greystonbakery.com), and at gourmet shops and restaurants around New York City. Greyston cakes have been served at venues as varied as the White House and Lincoln Center as well as everyday dining room tables around the country.

Each year, the bakery also makes 3 million pounds of brownies that are blended into several best-selling flavors of Ben & Jerry's ice creams and frozen yogurt. The Ben & Jerry's relationship exemplifies Greyston's position as a national pioneer of business collaboration for social impact. As a certified organic product producer and a certified kosher facility, the bakery is working to develop new baked products for Ben & Jerry's and also manufactures baked goods for Häagen-Dazs.

The bakery is still run by the charismatic Julius Walls Jr. Many bakery employees credit him with helping them turn their lives around. At the Greyston Bakery, the business model focuses on double bottom lines—financial success and sustainability—along with measurable social and personal transformation.

Walls is supported by a bakery board of directors that has included such highly regarded food experts as Rozanne Gold, winner of several James Beard awards for her *1-2-3 Cookbook* series; Michael Whiteman, preeminent restaurant developer of the Rainbow Room and Windows on the World; Michael Sands, former chief marketing officer for Snapple and founder of LesserEvil gourmet healthy treats; and Charles Lief, former president of the Greyston Foundation and author of two cookbooks. The bakery's social mission is supported by board member Amy Hall, manager of social accountability for Eileen Fisher clothing.

Most important, the bakery's sweet, unexpected success is still guided by the spiritually based values of compassion and service. Those who run the operation say it's all about the employees and the way their hard work complements the work done by the Greyston Foundation, enlivening the surrounding community.

The Greyston Mansion, with members of the Zen Community of New York (above)
The Monastery of the Blessed Sacrament, currently home of the Greyston Foundation offices (below)

Bernie Glassman and Sandra Jishu Holmes, founders of the Greyston Bakery,
and others from the Zen Community of New York

ᴄ❧

When the bakery began hiring local residents, it quickly became obvious that employment was just one of many unmet needs of the community. Most of these employees' résumés were filled with street life, drug addiction, and incarceration. Glassman and his late wife, Greyston cofounder, Sensei Sandra Jishu Holmes (herself an ordained Zen teacher educated as a molecular biologist), envisioned a nonprofit community development organization that would offer housing, jobs, social services, child care, and HIV-related health care.

In 1992, Greyston purchased a 19th-century former convent, the Monastery of the Blessed Sacrament, and its attached mansion (known as the Flagg Mansion). The convent sits less than a mile from the bakery, with views of the Hudson River. The newly formed Greyston Foundation made its offices there, sharing the space with the last of the convent's nuns. This unusual cohabitation between the Buddhists and the Catholic nuns provided an eclectic, deeply rooted spiritual backdrop to the services Greyston provided to the community.

It has always been clear that most of those whom Greyston serves are not Buddhist, and most have Christianity as their spiritual reference point. While Greyston continues to celebrate its Buddhist heritage, the foundation never imposes Buddhist theology on the community. The Buddhist values that inform Greyston's work are also the core spiritual values shared by most other faiths. It is in this way that Greyston supports people as they pursue their own paths. The grand chapel of the former convent still hosts a variety of meditation sessions, Sunday morning Christian services, Islamic celebrations, interfaith events, weddings and funerals, and even a by-appointment-only thrift store run by the participants in Greyston's HIV programs.

In the mid-1990s, Glassman left Yonkers to pursue other endeavors, and Greyston was faced with the challenges inherent to any organization facing a departing charismatic founder. But it thrived. With new leadership, Greyston reorganized under the notion of the *mandala* (a Sanskrit word meaning "circle" or "whole") as a guiding principle for community activities and services.

Flagg Mansion, currently home of the Greyston Foundation offices (above)
The chapel at the Monastery of the Blessed Sacrament (below)

Greyston's efforts to provide basic needs for the surrounding community reflect this circular shape, and that organization is mirrored by the cakes and tarts made by the bakery.

Today, in addition to the bakery, the Greyston mandala encompasses the following six programs:

Supportive Housing: About 150 units with in-house support services for formerly homeless and very low-income working families.

Greyston Health Services: Residence, day-program, and alternative treatments for people with HIV/AIDS.

Affordable Housing: Housing for low-income seniors, artists, volunteer fire and ambulance corps members, teachers, and others who need affordable living spaces if they are to remain in the community. This housing is located in the Burnham Building in nearby Irvington, New York, and in Philipsburgh Hall in Yonkers (which also houses a not-for-profit performing arts center). Both buildings, refurbished by Greyston, are on the National Register of Historic Places.

Child Care Center: Affordable care for 80 children, some of whose parents are bakery employees, in downtown Yonkers.

Youth Programs: Includes a youth enterprise and business skills program for school-age children. Recently, the program participants successfully marketed a line of gourmet lollipops.

Community Garden Project: Gardens on formerly blighted plots of Yonkers land. The garden project brings together more than 1,500 people each year, from preschool classes to seniors, and offer hands-on ecological education and family plots for raising vegetables.

With a $13 million annual operating budget, the foundation's programs employ 180 people and provide intensive services to more than 1,200 people each year. Thousands more are served through the community gardens and other smaller, seasonal programs.

The bakery and foundation have grown tremendously since the day, 25 years ago, when the Zen community of New York opened its little café to sell baked goods to the neighborhood. Though most of the original Buddhists have left, and there is no predawn meditation session, the basic tenet of right livelihood—that which brings true benefit to oneself and others—still guides the work done at both organizations. Whether it means training recently hired hard-to-employ community members to bake brownies for Ben & Jerry's, providing integrated services to people with HIV, or creating affordable housing, Greyston feeds the community a sweet supreme meal, and it is all done with the principle of right livelihood guiding the way.

The main part of this book features recipes for Greyston's popular desserts and many others inspired by the way Greyston bakes: simply and sweetly. These recipes are for the home kitchen, where it feels best to bake and to eat.

The book also covers a collection of basic recipes: vanilla and chocolate chiffon layer cake recipes referred to many times in the Cakes chapter, along with a few basic frostings to try on the cakes; a basic tart crust you'll use for most of the tarts in the book; and toppings such as Caramel Sauce and Spiked Whipped Cream, which are suggested as complements in many of the recipes. These recipes form a basic baking arsenal: Master them and you can bake dozens of different desserts.

As you read and cook with these recipes, I hope you absorb the powerful and heartfelt vision of the Greyston family and its 25-year history.

WELCOME TO OUR KITCHEN.

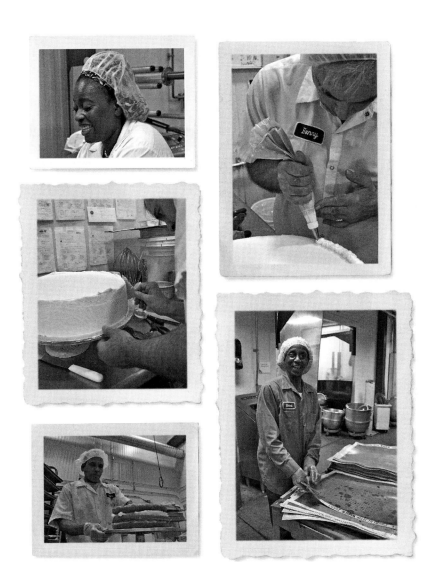

Greyston Bakery employees (above)

Getting Started

Before we get to the recipes, it's important to familiarize yourself with the basics. In this chapter, I'll explain some particulars for ingredients and equipment as well as some tips for decorating your finished baked desserts. When cooking with the recipes that follow, it's very important that you read the entire recipe before beginning. This simple step will ensure that you have the ingredients you need and that you've completed the necessary prep work.

INGREDIENTS

THE QUALITY OF YOUR INGREDIENTS WILL PLAY A BIG PART IN YOUR FINISHED BAKED GOODS. WHEN POSSIBLE, USE ALL-NATURAL AND ORGANIC PRODUCTS. THINK OF YOUR INGREDIENTS AS YOUR FOUNDATION; A HEALTHY, HIGH-QUALITY FOUNDATION WILL INEVITABLY GIVE YOU A HEAD START TOWARD A SUCCESSFUL RESULT. BELOW, I'VE LISTED INFORMATION ON SOME BAKING STAPLES AND MY PREFERRED FORMS AND BRANDS.

* * *

BAKING POWDER

A combination of baking soda and an acid, baking powder is a leavening agent that helps baked goods rise and stay fluffy. Double-acting baking powder, which is the most widely available variety, has two acidic ingredients so that gas is released when exposed to moisture during the mixing process and when exposed to heat during the baking process. Baking powder should be kept in a tightly sealed container to protect it from moisture. Properly stored, baking powder lasts about 1 year. To test if it's still good, mix a teaspoon of it with a few table-spoons of hot water. If it doesn't bubble, it's time for a new tin.

BAKING SODA

Also known as sodium bicarbonate, baking soda is another leavening agent. It gives off carbon dioxide when combined with an acid, so you'll see it used in rec-ipes containing some kind of mildly acidic ingredient such as chocolate, citrus juices, buttermilk, or brown sugar. Even in the traditional cardboard box, an open container of baking soda will last indefinitely. However, because many pan-tries can be dusty, I like to buy baking soda in the plastic container or transfer a new box of it to my own container.

BUTTER

Be sure to read a recipe before beginning, to determine how to prepare the butter you'll be using. For example, when making tart crusts, it is essential that the butter—along with all of the ingredients—is very cold. To ensure the butter is cold enough, cut it into small pieces and place them in the freezer for 10 minutes before using. Most other recipes call for butter "softened to room temperature." This is no joke. The best way to soften butter is to slice it into tablespoon-size tiles and set them out in your kitchen for at least 30 minutes. Quick methods such as setting the butter on the stove over the pilot light or running it through the microwave on low will give disastrously uneven results. When baking, I recommend sticking with unsalted butter so that you can control the total amount of salt in each recipe.

BUTTERMILK

Buttermilk is a wonderful tool in baking because it makes recipes moister and adds a nice tangy flavor. If you don't have buttermilk on hand, a fairly good substitute is a mixture of 1 teaspoon of fresh lemon juice and 1 cup of whole milk for every cup of buttermilk called for in a recipe.

CHOCOLATE

These days, there are myriad chocolates available for baking. Most of the recipes in this book call for semisweet or bittersweet chocolate. These chocolates can contain from 35 percent to more than 70 percent chocolate liquor (also called cacao). Imported chocolate bars often state the percentage right on the label, but most American brands do not. The key is to use chocolate of the highest quality you can afford. A cake made with Valrhona, Lindt, or Scharffen Berger chocolate will taste different than a cake made with bars of Hershey's semisweet baking chocolate. Taste chocolates and see which you like best. If budget is a consideration, save the finer stuff for more concentrated chocolate recipes such as Chocolate Molten Cakelets (see page 72) or any recipe with a ganache filling or frosting.

COCOA

Unsweetened cocoa is called for in many of the recipes in this book. In Dutch-process (alkalized) cocoa, the acidity in the cocoa has been reduced, rendering it milder in flavor and slightly darker in color than natural cocoa. Natural cocoa (nonalkalized) has not gone through this process and imparts a stronger, more acidic flavor and a lighter color. The recipes in this book were developed with organic Dutch-process baking cocoa from Equal Exchange (see Directory of Sources on page 185). For your own baking, try experimenting with both varieties to see which you prefer. There is no scientific reason to use one over the other; it simply comes down to a flavor and color preference.

CREAM

Cream is labeled "heavy cream," "whipping cream," and sometimes "double cream." These terms are interchangeable, although in some brands, "heavy cream" is slightly higher in fat and thus will whip up faster and thicker.

EGGS

The recipes in this book were tested with large organic eggs. Substituting jumbo, extra-large, or medium eggs may affect the finished results. Of course, you are free to substitute large nonorganic eggs, but I encourage you, if it's within your budget, to support farms that use organic methods—or free-range, at the very least.

Most baking is best done with eggs at room temperature because a cold egg can result in reduced volume. Either remove the eggs from the refrigerator 1 hour before using them or, to quickly bring them to room temperature, immerse them (in their shells) in a bowl of very warm tap water for a few minutes.

Sometimes a recipe calls for just egg whites or just egg yolks. If you find yourself with extra whites or yolks, save them for a later use. Whites can be frozen for up to a year either individually in ice cube trays or in quantity in a freezer-safe container. They can be refrigerated, if tightly covered, for up to 4 days. If freezing yolks, add ½ teaspoon of sugar per yolk to keep them from becoming sticky once defrosted. (Decrease the amount of sugar in the recipe accordingly.) Yolks can be refrigerated for up to 3 days, covered in water in a tightly sealed container.

When storing in quantity, make sure to label the container so you know how many whites or yolks are inside. On average, a large egg contains 2 tablespoons of egg white and 1 tablespoon of egg yolk.

FLOUR

The recipes in this book were tested with unbleached all-purpose flour, except where noted. I like the widely available King Arthur brand (see Directory of Sources on page 185) because the flour is not artificially bleached or enhanced.

SALT

When baking, use fine grain (table) salt, not kosher or other coarse salts.

SUGAR, BROWN

Most of the recipes in this book call for light brown, rather than dark brown, sugar. Do not make a special trip to buy light if you have only the dark variety, but know that dark brown sugar will impart a more intense molasses flavor.

To keep brown sugar from hardening, store it in an airtight plastic container, or place a clay Brown Sugar Bear (www.sugarbearsinc.com) or other similar brown sugar saver in the container you are using for storage. They cost about $3 and will extend the shelf life of your brown sugar considerably.

SUGAR, CONFECTIONERS'

Also known as powdered sugar or 10x, confectioners' sugar is regular granulated sugar ground to a superfine powder and mixed with a small amount of cornstarch to prevent lumping. It is commonly used to make frostings, and its powdery texture works beautifully to dust decoratively across the top of desserts. Store it in an airtight container or plastic bag to prevent exposure to moisture.

SUGAR, GRANULATED

When a recipe calls for sugar, it means granulated sugar. These days, grocery stores offer a wide variety of sugars that can be used for baking, and if your budget allows, I recommend using organic, unrefined, or natural sugar. Regularly processed white sugar is refined and bleached, which you just don't need in everyday baking. I have had wonderful results using unrefined organic sugar. If, however, you do not have the budget for or access to these products, you will have success using regular white table sugar with all of the recipes in this book.

VANILLA

Stick to pure vanilla extract as opposed to vanilla flavoring. There are a variety of specialty vanillas on the market: Bourbon vanilla is from Madagascar and has a subtle flavor, while Tahitian vanilla has a more floral flavor. For the purposes of the home baker, regular store-brand vanilla—as long as it's labeled "pure vanilla extract"—will do.

EQUIPMENT

THERE IS A CERTAIN, ALBEIT SMALL, AMOUNT OF EQUIPMENT NECESSARY FOR BAKING: AN OVEN AND A FEW PANS, AT THE VERY LEAST. FROM THERE, YOU CAN ADD A VARIETY OF ITEMS TO YOUR ARSENAL THAT MAKE BAKING MUCH FASTER, EASIER, AND MORE CONVENIENT. READ EACH RECIPE IN ITS ENTIRETY BEFORE SETTING OUT TO MAKE IT. IF THERE IS A PARTICULAR PIECE OF EQUIPMENT THAT SEEMS ESSENTIAL, BUT YOU'D RATHER NOT BUY IT, START KNOCKING ON NEIGHBORS' DOORS OR CALL YOUR FRIENDS OR FAMILY. YOU'D BE SURPRISED AT WHAT SOME PEOPLE KEEP IN THE FAR REACHES OF THEIR KITCHEN CABINETS.

CAKE STAND

To frost a cake comfortably, it helps to raise it closer to eye level. Being able to turn the cake makes this task even easier. Cake decorating turntables made by companies such as Wilton (see Directory of Sources on page 185) and Ateco are available at kitchenware and restaurant supply stores.

If you'd rather not add a cake stand to your baking collection, use a flat platter whose diameter is at least 2" larger than the cake. Place strips of parchment or waxed paper underneath the cake before frosting. You can carefully pull the strips away after the frosting is applied, leaving behind a clean surface.

CAKE STRIPS

No matter how closely you follow a recipe, it is virtually impossible to bake a cake without it coming out of the oven with an elevated center—and when you're making layer cakes, it ends up being sliced off and wasted. To avoid this problem, there is a wonderful invention called a cake strip (Bake Even Strips or Magi-Cake Strips), which is a fabric strip coated with aluminum that you moisten and wrap around a cake pan. The insulation the strip provides helps to maintain moisture throughout the baking process, eliminating peaked centers, cracked tops, and crusty edges. Cake strips come in a variety of sizes. One pair of 30"-long strips gets me through all my baking, and it will certainly cover you for any of the recipes in this book.

Alternatively, you can make your own cake strips. Dampen a dish towel and fold it until it is a narrow strip as wide as your pan is high. Then just tie it around the pan. Check the pan occasionally as you bake to ensure that the towel doesn't burn.

COOLING RACKS

Two racks are better than one. If you make cookies or layer cakes, or find yourself on a baking spree, you'll be glad you have this extra landing space for your recipes to cool evenly.

DECORATING COMB

If you like the scored look often seen on the sides of carrot cakes and other traditional frosted cakes, you'll want a decorating comb. This triangular metal tool is easy to use. Just drag the edge across the frosting to make straight, zigzag, or other combed patterns.

DOUBLE BOILER

Very few of us have actual double boilers, but one can easily be fashioned out of a saucepan and a heatproof glass or metal bowl. The important thing is to get the sizes right. The bowl should rest on top of the saucepan—not inside of it. If you are melting chocolate, choose a wider bowl to melt the chocolate more evenly. Make sure the saucepan is large enough so that when it holds a few inches of simmering water and the bowl is placed on top of it, only steam, and not water, touches the bottom of the bowl.

FOOD PROCESSOR

A food processor, such as a Cuisinart, makes pastry dough assembly much more efficient than the hand method, although it is neither impossible nor unpleasant to use the hand method. (I rather enjoy getting my hands deep into a crust.) If you choose to work by hand, be sure to work quickly because the introduction of anything warm, including fingers and palms, can negatively affect a pastry dough. A food processor is also useful for grinding nuts and wafer cookies such as graham crackers, which are used in some cheesecake and tart crusts.

OFFSET SPATULA

An offset spatula has a blade that tilts up where it meets the handle and is a must-have for frosting cakes. The shape allows your wrist to move naturally and comfortably.

OVEN

You can use either an electric or gas oven. For small batches of cookies, I've even used a toaster oven. Make sure to bake with the rack in the centermost position, unless otherwise directed. If baking more than one dish at a time, leave 2" of space around all sides of the pans.

OVEN THERMOMETER

Ovens vary enormously. Having a thermometer to tell you where your oven falls in the grand scheme of oven temperatures will be helpful. You should test your oven at several different temperatures to make sure it's accurately calibrated.

PANS

To make most of the desserts in this book, you'll need just a few pans. First, you'll need 9" and 10" cake pans with removable bottoms or a springform pan, also called a cheesecake pan. The sides of these pans should be at least 2" high. You will need two 8" cake pans with 1" to 1½" sides for layer cakes and one 10" pan for single-layer cakes. There are a few cake recipes that call for a Bundt pan, or tube cake pan, or an angel food cake pan. These take up room on the shelf, so buy them only if you make these recipes often. Otherwise, borrow from a fellow baker.

For tarts, you'll need a 9" tart pan with a removable bottom and fluted edges.

For bars, you'll need one 9" x 13" x 2" baking pan and a 9" square pan. If you intend on making cookies, it's good to have more than one cookie sheet on hand so you can do several batches at a time.

All recipes have instructions for greasing and lining pans with parchment paper, and you should follow these instructions closely whether you use non-stick or regular pans. To keep desserts from sticking, it helps to add a dusting of flour once the pan is fitted with the parchment paper. Simply add a small spoonful and then rotate the pan to distribute the flour. When finished, tap out the excess.

It should be noted that nonstick pans, because of their darker color, tend to conduct heat more evenly than lighter pans, so if you use them, watch the time or try reducing the oven temperature by 25°F. Avoid flimsy and disposable metal pans, which bake unevenly, warp in the oven, and develop hot spots while baking.

PARCHMENT PAPER

Parchment paper makes baking easier. You still have to grease the pan, but lining it with parchment paper guarantees that you will not be scraping the pan when removing cakes or cookie bars. Parchment is available in rolls, precut sheets, and precut rounds. The rolls can be cumbersome, so I prefer to buy the sheets and cut the rounds myself. If you plan to do a lot of cake baking, you can buy a selection of rounds (8" and 10"), but if you are using the paper for cookies and bars as well, the rectangular sheets are the most efficient and economical.

PASTRY BAGS AND TIPS

If you want to get fancy and decorate cakes like a professional, you'll need a set of cloth or nylon pastry bags and metal or plastic tips. Note that cloth bags tend to crack and sometimes develop a sour smell after being used a few times, so a synthetic one might be more pleasant to keep around your kitchen. Ateco is the more commonly found brand of tips and usually sells sets—some small and simple, others quite elaborate—for cake decorating.

PIECRUST SHIELDS

When tarts have to bake for more than 30 minutes, there is a risk that the edges of the crust will brown too quickly. You can prevent this from happening by cutting out strips of aluminum foil each time you bake and carefully fitting them around the edges of the crust. Or you can invest about $3 in a set of piecrust shields made by Norpro. Each set has five adjustable and reusable aluminum strips that slip perfectly around the edge of a tart ring.

PIE WEIGHTS

Pie weights ensure that prebaked tart crusts bake evenly and without air pockets or shrinkage. You can buy pie weights either in the form of little ceramic marbles or as one stainless steel chain, similar to a Mardi Gras necklace. I prefer the stainless steel version since it is in one piece and is easier to handle and store. You can also substitute dry beans or rice, which will serve the same purpose. The pastry is always topped with parchment paper to begin, so no matter what the material, there is no contact between the dough and the weights.

RUBBER SPATULA

This simple tool is essential for getting extra batter or frosting from a bowl. The extra can amount to as much as $\frac{1}{4}$ cup, which makes a big difference in the finished product.

SCALE

Professional bakers weigh rather than manually measure their ingredients, and with practice, you will find that this method is more reliable than measuring. There are small, relatively inexpensive digital scales, such as those made by Salter, that don't take up very much shelf space. This is not an essential item, but once you have one, you will find yourself using it more than you expected.

SERRATED BREAD KNIFE

A bread knife that is at least 12" long is the perfect tool for slicing a cake into horizontal layers, as well as for shaving off an uneven top.

STAND MIXER

Although not a necessity for baking, an electric mixer makes life easier. Kitchen-Aid is the rig of choice for most home bakers. It makes creaming butter and cream cheese a breeze and makes batters that would require minutes of elbow grease to be smooth and pan-ready in just a few seconds. A good mixer is quite heavy and comes with at least three attachments. Two of them, the paddle and the whisk, are invaluable for dessert making. If you are baking a lot, it is wise to buy a second bowl, whisk, and paddle so that you do not have to bother with washing dishes between steps.

A new KitchenAid (5-quart size) runs about $300, although you can find good deals on barely used models through Web sites such as www.ebay.com and www.craigslist.com.

You can also use a portable, handheld electric mixer, which is still easier than working by hand, although it does not allow you to walk away while it does the work.

ZESTER

The most efficient way to get zest from the skin of a citrus fruit, without any of the bitter white pith, is to use a zester. I prefer the Microplane brand, though there are many other available models. It's a small investment for your kitchen arsenal that will give you lots of help—not only while zesting, but while grating fresh nutmeg and Parmesan cheese.

BAKING AT HIGH ALTITUDES

If you are baking at an altitude above 3,000 feet, certain modifications need to be made. You'll find it's harder to boil water, leavening agents will have more power, batters stick more to your pans, and sugar gets sweeter. To adjust, expect longer cooking times when boiling, raise the oven temperature by 25°F when baking, underbeat your eggs, and make the following specific ingredient changes.

Altitude (feet)	Reduce Each Teaspoon Baking Powder/Soda By	Reduce Each Cup Sugar By	Increase Each Cup Liquid By
3,000-5,000	$\frac{1}{8}$ teaspoon	1 tablespoon	2 tablespoons
5,000-7,000	$\frac{1}{8}$-$\frac{1}{4}$ teaspoon	2 tablespoons	2-3 tablespoons
7,000-10,000	$\frac{1}{4}$-$\frac{1}{2}$ teaspoon	2-3 tablespoons	3-4 tablespoons
10,000 and above	$\frac{1}{2}$-$\frac{2}{3}$ teaspoon	3-4 tablespoons	3-4 tablespoons

For more on the topic of high-altitude cooking, an excellent resource is Susan G. Purdy's book *Pie in the Sky* (Morrow/HarperCollins Publishers, 2005).

DECORATING TIPS AND TECHNIQUES

WHEN BAKING DESSERTS, A FEW EXTRA MINUTES SPENT DECORATING GO A VERY LONG WAY. THIS SECTION GIVES BASIC INSTRUCTIONS FOR ENSURING YOUR DESSERTS LOOK AS WONDERFUL AS THEY TASTE.

FROSTING A LAYER CAKE

Layer cakes are always crowd-pleasers—especially when they are beautifully frosted and decorated.

To frost a two-layer cake, begin by placing the bottom layer on a platter with three or four strips of waxed paper or parchment along the edges. Use an offset or straight spatula, ideally as long as the width of the cake, dipped in warm water and wiped clean after each application.

Brush the top and sides of the cake to remove any loose crumbs. Using the spatula, apply a very thin layer of frosting on the exposed surface to keep any extra crumbs down.

Set aside any frosting you will need to decorate the cake. Place half of the remaining frosting (or one-third, if you're frosting a three-layer cake) on the top surface of the first layer and spread it evenly. Push the frosting from the top down the sides with even strokes, turning the cake as you go. Place the second layer of cake on top, cut side down. Place the second half of the frosting on the top layer and frost as before, keeping the spatula parallel to the sides of the cake as you spread the frosting around the sides, again turning the cake as you go.

Once you are satisfied with the smoothness and evenness of the frosting, gently tug at the paper strips to remove them from the platter. You should have a clean surface to decorate or garnish, or from which to serve. Garnish with Candied Citrus Strips, Candied Citrus Slices, Chocolate Curls, or Chocolate Leaves. Recipes for these garnishes are found in Basic Recipes, beginning on page 29.

DECORATING WITH CONFECTIONERS' SUGAR AND COCOA

You can elegantly decorate cakes and tarts with a sprinkling of confectioners' sugar or cocoa, either freehand or using stencils.

To decorate freehand, sift either confectioners' sugar or cocoa over the top of the dessert with a fine-mesh sieve by holding it about 6" above the dessert and tapping the side of the sieve gently with the heel of your hand. Confectioners' sugar works best on dark cakes, such as chocolate, and cocoa works best on lighter cakes, such as those with a buttercream or whipped cream frosting.

To decorate using a stencil, place it as snugly as possible across the top surface of the dessert and sprinkle the sugar or cocoa with a sieve. You can purchase stencils (see Directory of Sources on page 185), or you can make your own with strips of parchment paper laid across the top of the dessert. Try crisscross patterns or get fancier by cutting out shapes such as stars, hearts, and polka dots.

Basic Recipes

In order to become a baking master, some people might attend culinary school and practice their skills rigorously. Most home bakers do not have such lofty goals or the time to make them happen. However, there are a few basic recipes you can include in your baking repertoire that will give you a leg up as a baker. Once you can make good vanilla and chocolate chiffon layer cakes, basic tart pastry, some icings, and a few finishing flourishes, you can begin to improvise with alternate flavorings and fillers. This chapter presents 17 recipes that will be referred to often in the recipe chapters of the book and are also a great place to start if you want to learn the basics of baking.

Vanilla Chiffon Cake Layers

Makes two 8" layers

5 eggs, separated
¼ cup (½ stick) unsalted butter,
   melted and cooled
½ cup milk
1½ teaspoons pure vanilla extract

1½ cups unbleached all-purpose flour
1¼ cups sugar
2½ teaspoons baking powder
¼ teaspoon salt

Position a rack in the center of the oven and preheat the oven to 350°F. Grease and flour two 8" round cake pans and line the pan bottoms with parchment paper rounds.

In a small bowl, combine the egg yolks, butter, milk, and vanilla. Set aside.

In a large bowl, whisk together the flour, 1 cup of the sugar, baking powder, and salt to blend. Add the egg yolk mixture and stir until well combined. Set aside.

In a clean dry bowl, using clean dry beaters, beat the egg whites on medium-high speed until they hold soft peaks. Lower the mixer speed to medium and gradually add the remaining ¼ cup sugar, beating the whites until they hold stiff peaks. Stir about one-third of the egg whites into the batter to lighten. Gently fold the remaining whites into the batter, in two batches, to blend thoroughly.

Transfer the batter to the prepared pans, filling them equally. Bake for 30 to 35 minutes, or until the sides of the cakes begin to pull away slightly from the pans and a wooden skewer inserted near the center of the cake comes out clean.

Set the pans on a wire rack for 10 minutes to cool. Turn out the cakes and carefully remove the parchment. Reinvert the cakes and allow them to cool completely on wire racks.

Chocolate Chiffon Cake Layers

Makes two 8" layers

6 eggs, separated
¾ cup vegetable oil
½ cup milk
1½ teaspoons pure vanilla extract
1 cup unbleached all-purpose flour

1½ cups sugar
¾ cup unsweetened cocoa
2 teaspoons baking powder
1 teaspoon baking soda
⅛ teaspoon salt

Position a rack in the center of the oven and preheat the oven to 350°F. Grease and flour two 8" round cake pans and line the pan bottoms with parchment paper rounds.

In a small bowl, combine the egg yolks, oil, milk, and vanilla. Set aside.

In a large bowl, whisk together the flour, 1 cup of the sugar, the cocoa powder, baking powder, baking soda, and salt to blend. Add the egg yolk mixture to the dry ingredients and stir to blend. Set aside.

In a clean dry bowl, using clean dry beaters, beat the egg whites on medium-high speed until they hold soft peaks. Lower the mixer speed to medium and gradually add the remaining ½ cup sugar, beating the whites until they form stiff peaks. Stir about one-third of the egg whites into the batter to lighten. Gently fold in the remaining whites, in two batches, to blend thoroughly.

Transfer the batter to the prepared pans, filling them equally. Bake for 30 to 35 minutes, or until the sides of the cakes begin to pull away slightly from the pans and a wooden skewer inserted near the center of the cake comes out clean.

Set the pans on a wire rack for 10 minutes to cool. Turn out the cakes and carefully remove the parchment. Reinvert the cakes and allow them to cool completely on wire racks.

Tart Pastry

Makes one 9" tart shell, plus a small amount leftover

1¼ cups unbleached all-purpose flour
2 tablespoons sugar
¼ teaspoon salt

7 tablespoons unsalted butter, cut
    into very small pieces and chilled
1–3 tablespoons ice water (or as
    needed)

BY HAND

In a bowl, whisk together the flour, sugar, and salt to blend thoroughly. Using a pastry blender, metal pastry scraper, two knives, or your fingers, cut or rub the butter into the dry ingredients until the mixture resembles a coarse meal. (Work quickly to keep the butter cold.)

Using a fork, stir in the water, 1 tablespoon at a time, adding just enough for the dough to hold together without becoming wet. Gather the dough into a ball and then flatten it into a disk. Wrap the disk of dough in plastic wrap and chill for 1 hour.

WITH FOOD PROCESSOR

In the work bowl of a food processor fitted with a metal blade, combine the flour, sugar, and salt. Add the butter and process, using short pulses, until the mixture resembles a coarse meal.

With the machine running, add the water through the feed tube, 1 tablespoon at a time, until the dough begins to form into a ball. Remove the dough from the food processor and flatten into a disk. Wrap the disk of dough in plastic wrap and chill for 1 hour.

FORM THE SHELL

Remove the dough from the refrigerator. Using a rolling pin on a lightly floured board, roll the dough to form a rough circle about ¼" thick. Carefully transfer the dough to a 9" fluted tart pan with a removable bottom. Press the dough lightly but snugly into the edges of the pan, allowing the excess dough to hang over the edges of the pan. Roll the rolling pin over the top of the pan to trim the excess dough from the pan rim. Pierce the bottom of the dough several times with the tines of a fork. Chill for at least 30 minutes before baking.

The tart shell is now ready to either bake, partially bake, or freeze for up to 1 month for future use. If freezing, wrap tightly with plastic wrap, taking care to press the plastic against the surface of the dough.

FOR A FULLY BAKED SHELL

Position a rack in the center of the oven and preheat the oven to 400°F. Line the chilled shell with foil or parchment and fill with pie weights, dried beans, or raw rice.

Bake the shell for 12 minutes, or until the pastry is set and golden. Carefully remove the foil or parchment and weights and continue to bake the shell another 10 to 15 minutes, or until the pastry is golden brown. If the edges start to brown too much, cover them with strips of foil or piecrust shields (see page 9). Cool on a rack.

FOR A PARTIALLY BAKED SHELL

Position a rack in the center of the oven and preheat the oven to 400°F. Line the chilled shell with foil or parchment and fill the shell with pie weights, dried beans, or raw rice.

Bake the shell for 12 minutes, or until the pastry is set and golden. Carefully remove the foil or parchment and weights and continue to bake the shell another 5 minutes, or until it is golden all over. If the edges of the shell start to brown too much, cover them with strips of foil or piecrust shields (see page 9). Cool on a rack.

WHAT TO DO WITH LEFTOVER TART PASTRY

If you find yourself with extra tart dough after rolling out your pastry, don't toss it out. Gather the scraps together into a ball and roll it out into a small circle. Fill the circle with any combination of fruit preserves, fresh sliced fruit, chopped nuts, butter and brown sugar, or cream cheese. Tuck up the sides to form a pouch and bake the pouch at 350°F for 5 to 10 minutes, or until the pastry begins to brown.

Vanilla Butter Cream Frosting

Makes about 3 cups, enough to frost an 8" double-layer cake

½ cup (1 stick) unsalted butter,
   softened to room temperature
4 cups (about one 1-pound package)
   confectioners' sugar, sifted

¼ cup heavy cream
1½ teaspoons pure vanilla extract

In the bowl of an electric mixer, beat the butter at medium speed until creamy. Reduce the speed to low and gradually add 2 cups of the confectioners' sugar and ⅛ cup of the cream, beating at low speed until blended. Add the remaining 2 cups sugar and ⅛ cup cream. Continue to beat on low speed until blended. Add the vanilla and beat until blended.

Chocolate Butter Cream Frosting

Makes about 3 cups, enough to frost an 8" double-layer cake

4 ounces good-quality bittersweet or semisweet chocolate, finely chopped

½ cup (1 stick) unsalted butter, softened to room temperature

4 cups (about one 1-pound package) confectioners' sugar, sifted

¼ cup heavy cream

Melt the chocolate in a double boiler. Let cool to room temperature.

In the bowl of an electric mixer, beat the butter at medium speed until creamy. Reduce the speed to low and gradually add 2 cups of the confectioners' sugar and ⅛ cup of the cream, beating at low speed until blended. Add the remaining 2 cups sugar and ⅛ cup cream. Continue to beat on low speed until blended. Gradually pour in the cooled chocolate and beat until blended.

Apricot Glaze

Makes about ½ cup

½ cup apricot preserves

2 tablespoons water or orange-flavored liqueur such as Cointreau or Triple Sec

In a small saucepan, bring the preserves and water (or liqueur) to a boil over medium heat, stirring often. Cook 2 to 3 minutes, or until thickened. If the preserves contain large chunks of fruit, transfer the glaze to a blender or food processor and process until smooth. Strain the glaze through a mesh sieve into a small bowl, pressing the glaze with the back of a large spoon or rubber spatula to extract as much liquid as possible. Use while still warm.

Red Currant Glaze

Makes about ½ cup

½ cup red currant jelly

2 tablespoons water or berry liqueur such as kirsch or framboise

In a small saucepan, bring the jelly and water (or liqueur) to a boil over medium heat, stirring often. Cook 2 to 3 minutes, or until thickened. Use while still warm.

Simple Syrup

Makes about ½ cup

½ cup water
¼ cup sugar

2 tablespoons kirsch or other fruit-
flavored liqueur (optional)

In a small saucepan with a lid, combine the water and sugar and stir over medium heat until the sugar dissolves and the mixture comes to a boil. Cover, remove from heat, and allow the syrup to cool completely. Stir in the liqueur, if using.

Caramel Sauce

Makes about 1 cup

1 cup sugar

¾ cup water

1 cup heavy cream

In a medium saucepan, combine the sugar and water and stir over medium heat, dissolving the sugar and bringing the mixture to a boil. Continue to cook, stirring and occasionally swirling the pan and brushing down the sides of the pan with a wet pastry brush. Cook for 10 minutes, or until the mixture turns a deep caramel color.

Remove the pan from the heat. Slowly add the cream and whisk to combine. Return the sauce to low heat, stirring until the sauce becomes completely smooth.

Remove the sauce from the heat and serve warm or at room temperature. If not using the sauce immediately, cover and refrigerate for up to 2 weeks. To reheat, warm the sauce over medium-low heat until it reaches a pourable consistency. Serve warm or let the sauce cool to room temperature.

Whipped Cream

Makes about 2 cups

1 cup heavy cream, well-chilled

Chill a mixing bowl and whisk attachment in the freezer for 15 minutes. Pour the cream into the chilled bowl and beat on low speed for 30 seconds, or until small bubbles form. Gradually increase the mixer speed to high. Continue whipping on high speed until the cream has doubled in volume and forms stiff peaks. Cover the whipped cream and refrigerate for up to 24 hours. If the cream separates, whisk it by hand until it comes back together.

Note: If whipping by hand, it helps to have a stainless steel balloon whisk, which has a more bulbous whisk head than a regular whisk.

Spiked Whipped Cream

Makes about 2 cups

1 cup heavy cream, well-chilled
3 tablespoons confectioners' sugar

2 tablespoons liqueur or spirits of your choice, such as Grand Marnier, Cointreau, rum, framboise, kirsch, cassis, or Cognac

Chill a mixing bowl and whisk attachment in the freezer for 15 minutes. Pour the cream into the chilled bowl and beat on low speed for 30 seconds, or until small bubbles form. Gradually increase the mixer speed to high. When the cream starts to form soft peaks, add the confectioners' sugar and liqueur or spirits and continue whipping on high speed until the cream has doubled in volume and forms stiff peaks. Cover the whipped cream and refrigerate for up to 24 hours. If the cream separates, whisk it by hand until it comes back together.

Note: *If whipping by hand, it helps to have a stainless steel balloon whisk, which has a more bulbous whisk head than a regular whisk.*

Crème Fraîche

Makes about 1 cup

---

1 cup heavy cream   2 tablespoons buttermilk

Combine the cream and buttermilk in a glass container. Cover the container and let stand at room temperature for at least 8 hours (or up to 24 hours). When the crème fraîche becomes thick, like sour cream, stir well. Refrigerate for up to 10 days.

Candied Citrus Strips

Candied Citrus Strips are a nice touch to any cake that contains citrus. They can be stored at room temperature in an airtight container for about a month.

Citrus fruit (such as 2 lemons,
   1 medium orange, 1 grapefruit,
   or 3 limes)

1 cup + 3 tablespoons sugar
½ cup water

Thoroughly wash the fruit. With a small paring knife or vegetable peeler, cut slices of peel, leaving the white pith behind. Stack the strips on a cutting board and cut them into ¼"-wide pieces.

Over medium-high heat, bring a small saucepan of water to a boil and cook the strips for 5 minutes, or until they become limp. If cooking enough to crowd the pan, use a larger saucepan or boil the peel in batches.

Meanwhile, in another saucepan, combine 1 cup sugar and the water and bring to a boil over medium heat, stirring until the sugar is dissolved. Add the strips, reduce the heat to a low simmer, and cook for 30 minutes, or until the strips have lost much of their color. Carefully remove the strips from the syrup with a slotted spoon, and allow them to dry on a sheet of waxed paper for several hours or overnight.

Place 3 tablespoons sugar in a wide bowl or lipped dessert plate or saucer and toss the strips in the sugar.

Candied Citrus Slices

A wafer-thin slice of candied lime, orange, or lemon is another beautiful garnish to a cake or tart containing citrus.

Citrus fruit (such as 1 small orange, 1 lemon, or 2 limes)

1 cup sugar
1 cup water

Thoroughly wash the fruit. Slice the fruit as thin and evenly as possible. (A mandoline helps with this task.)

Bring the sugar and water to a boil in a small skillet or saucepan over medium heat. When the sugar is dissolved, reduce the heat to a simmer and add the sliced fruit in a single layer. Cook the fruit for 30 minutes, turning a few times to ensure it cooks evenly. Remove the slices with a slotted spoon and cool completely on a wire rack.

Candied Citrus Slices will keep for several days stored in an airtight container, with layers separated by sheets of waxed paper.

Chocolate Curls

It's easiest to make Chocolate Curls for garnishes when the chocolate is warm. To warm your chocolate, microwave it for a few seconds on low power or wrap it in a dish towel and place it in a very low oven (200°F or less) for 3 to 5 minutes.

Block of good-quality semisweet chocolate, slightly warmed

Line a baking sheet with waxed paper or parchment.

With a very sharp knife, scrape the warm chocolate at a 45-degree angle, or drag a vegetable peeler across the side of the block, applying sufficient pressure to bring up enough chocolate to hold a curl. Gently move each curl to the prepared baking sheet. Refrigerate, covered with plastic wrap, until ready to use.

Chocolate Leaves

It is best to prepare a few more leaves than you need as the chocolate may break or melt during handling.

....

24 smooth, firm, veined leaves with stems (see note)

4 ounces chopped chocolate

....

Wipe the leaves clean with a damp cloth and then let dry thoroughly.

Meanwhile, line a baking sheet with waxed paper and set aside.

Melt the chocolate in the top of a double boiler set over medium heat, stirring until smooth. (Alternatively, melt the chocolate in a microwave oven in a micro-waveable bowl on medium power, checking and stirring after 1 minute, and then checking and stirring every 10 to 20 seconds, until completely melted.)

Using a small pastry brush and holding the leaf by its stem, coat the veined side (underside) of each leaf with an even layer of chocolate. Set each leaf, chocolate side up, on the prepared baking sheet. When all of the leaves are coated, place the cookie sheet in the refrigerator until the chocolate hardens.

Remove the baking sheet from the refrigerator. Very carefully, peel the leaves away from the chocolate. Discard the leaves and return the chocolate leaves to the refrigerator until you are ready to use them. Chocolate leaves can be kept refrigerated in an airtight container for up to 2 days.

Note: *Good options for chocolate leaves include citrus, camellia, rose, or mint leaves. When using mint leaves, take extra care not to touch the chocolate when peeling the leaf away, because the chocolate may crumble. You can use tweezers to grasp the chocolate layer of each leaf and peel away the mint leaf by holding the stem end.*

Toasted Crumb Garnish

When making a layer cake, you'll need to trim the top of each cake to create a flat surface. Scraps from a chocolate layer cake are especially useful for decorating a finished cake—if you decide not to nibble on them!

....

Cake scraps from a layer cake

....

Position a rack in the center of the oven and preheat the oven to 375°F. Line a baking sheet with parchment paper.

Place the cake scraps on the prepared baking sheet and toast them in the oven for 15 minutes. Remove the baking sheet from the oven, and carefully break up the scraps with your fingers or a spatula. Return the baking sheet to the oven for 5 to 10 minutes longer, or until the crumbs are lightly toasted.

Remove the pan from the oven and allow the crumbs to cool completely. Break up any remaining clumps.

These crumbs can be patted in a ring pattern around the bottom of a frosted layer cake or on the sides or top of the cake for a textured look.

Cakes

When you bake a cake, it is usually to make an offering. Cakes are baked for birthday parties, dinner gatherings, and other celebrations. They are almost always tied to a community event of some sort. So it is fitting that Greyston, a place anchored in community, is known for its cakes. It is a community that bakes them, and it is communities like yours and mine that enjoy them. With the following recipes, we hope to keep that spirit alive. Of course, if any of these recipes seem so tantalizing that you decide to just bake one for yourself alone, we'll understand.

New York Cheesecake

Makes one 9" cake, 10–12 servings

The Greyston Bakery is known for its incredible cheesecake. This version has a graham cracker crumb crust and both lemon peel and lemon juice, which is known as New York style. Here, we offer both a plain version and one decadently glazed in chocolate ganache. (Photo page 149)

FOR THE CRUST
2¼ cups graham cracker crumbs (from about eighteen 2½" x 5" crackers)
¼ cup sugar
½ cup (1 stick) unsalted butter, melted

FOR THE FILLING
2 (8-ounce) packages cream cheese, softened to room temperature

1 cup sugar
¼ teaspoon salt
4 eggs
½ cup heavy cream
1 tablespoon grated lemon peel
2 tablespoons freshly squeezed lemon juice

PREPARE THE CRUST

Position a rack in the center of the oven and preheat the oven to 350°F.

In a bowl, mix the graham cracker crumbs, sugar, and butter until the crumbs are evenly moistened. Press the mixture onto the bottom and two-thirds of the way up the sides of a 9" round springform pan. Bake 10 to 15 minutes, or until the crust begins to deepen in color. Set the pan on a wire rack to cool. Reduce the oven temperature to 325°F.

PREPARE THE FILLING AND ASSEMBLE THE CHEESECAKE

In the bowl of an electric mixer, beat the cream cheese on medium speed until fluffy. Gradually beat in the sugar and salt. Add the eggs, one at a time, beating well after each addition. Beat in the cream, lemon peel, and lemon juice. Pour the mixture into the cooled crust.

Place the springform pan in a roasting pan and pour in enough hot water to come halfway up the sides of the springform pan. Bake 1½ hours, or until the filling is puffy and golden on top but still jiggles slightly when gently shaken. Remove the springform pan from the water and cool on a wire rack at least 1 hour, then refrigerate at least 6 hours. Let the cake stand at room temperature for 20 minutes before serving.

The cheesecake will keep, covered and refrigerated, for up to 3 days.

FOR A CHOCOLATE-GLAZED CHEESECAKE

8 ounces good-quality semisweet chocolate
½ cup water

2 tablespoons corn syrup
½ egg, lightly beaten

In a small heavy saucepan, combine the chocolate and water. Set over low heat, stirring constantly until the chocolate is completely melted and the mixture is smooth. Stir in the corn syrup and egg. Allow the mixture to cool slightly, then gently pour it over the cooled cheesecake. Chill for 1 hour, or until the glaze is set.

Cheesecake on the Lighter Side

Makes one 10" cake, about 16 servings

Here is a lighter version of the New York Cheesecake. It is best made a day ahead and chilled in the refrigerator overnight.

FOR THE CRUST

1 cup graham cracker crumbs (nine
  2½" x 5" crackers, crushed)
1 tablespoon sugar
2 tablespoons unsalted butter, melted

FOR THE FILLING

5 egg whites
1 whole egg
2 teaspoons pure vanilla extract

¼ teaspoon salt
1 tablespoon grated lemon zest
1 (15-ounce) container low-fat ricotta
  cheese, warmed to room
  temperature
2 (8-ounce) packages fat-free cream
  cheese, softened to room
  temperature
1 (8-ounce) container light sour cream
1 cup sugar

PREPARE THE CRUST

Position a rack in the center of the oven and preheat the oven to 400°F.

In a bowl, mix the graham cracker crumbs, sugar, and butter until the crumbs are evenly moistened. Press the mixture onto the bottom of a 10" round spring-form pan. Bake the crust for 10 minutes. Remove from the oven and cool on a wire rack. Reduce the oven temperature to 350°F.

PREPARE THE FILLING AND ASSEMBLE THE CHEESECAKE

In a mixing bowl, whisk the egg whites, whole egg, vanilla, and salt to blend. Stir in the lemon zest. Set aside.

In the bowl of an electric mixer, beat the ricotta cheese, cream cheese, and sour cream on medium speed until fluffy. Add the sugar and beat until combined. Add the egg mixture and mix to combine. Pour the batter over the cooled crust. Set the springform pan in a large roasting pan and pour in enough hot water to come halfway up the sides of the springform pan.

Bake 1 hour, or until the top is light golden and the filling jiggles only slightly when gently shaken. Remove the pan from the water and let it cool on a wire rack at least 1 hour, then refrigerate at least 6 hours before serving. Let the cake stand at room temperature for 20 minutes before serving.

The cheesecake will keep, covered and refrigerated, for up to 3 days.

Chocolate Chip Cheesecake

Makes one 9" cake, 10–12 servings

This cheesecake has a chocolate crumb crust and is dotted with mini chocolate chips throughout. A thin wedge of it is delicious with a cold glass of milk as an afternoon snack, and, of course, a more substantial slice is always welcome after dinner.

FOR THE CRUST

2¼ cups chocolate wafer crumbs
  (about 18 wafers, crushed)
½ cup (1 stick) unsalted butter, melted

FOR THE FILLING

2 (8-ounce) packages cream cheese,
  softened to room temperature

¾ cup sugar
3 eggs
½ cup heavy cream
2 teaspoons pure vanilla extract
¾ cup miniature semisweet chocolate
  chips

PREPARE THE CRUST

Position a rack in the center of the oven and preheat the oven to 350°F.

In a mixing bowl, mix the chocolate wafer crumbs and butter until the crumbs are evenly moistened. Press the mixture onto the bottom and two-thirds of the way up the sides of a 9" round springform pan. Bake 5 minutes. Remove the pan from the oven and let it cool on a wire rack. Reduce the oven temperature to 325°F.

PREPARE THE FILLING AND ASSEMBLE THE CHEESECAKE

In the bowl of an electric mixer, beat the cream cheese on medium speed until fluffy. Gradually add the sugar, beating well to combine. Add the eggs, one at a time, beating well after each addition. Add the cream and vanilla, and continue beating to combine. Remove the bowl from the mixer and stir in the chocolate chips by hand.

Pour the batter into the prepared crust. Place the springform pan in a roasting pan and pour in enough hot water to come halfway up the side of the springform pan. Bake 1¼ hours, or until the filling is puffy and golden on top but still jiggles slightly when gently shaken. Remove the springform pan from the water. Cool the pan on a wire rack at least 1 hour, then refrigerate for at least 6 hours.

Let the cake stand at room temperature for 20 minutes before serving. The cheesecake will keep, covered and refrigerated, for up to 3 days.

Pumpkin Praline Cheesecake

Makes one 10" cake, about 16 servings

This cheesecake makes a dazzling holiday alternative to traditional pumpkin pie, and you'll get more servings out of it than you would get out of a pie.

FOR THE PRALINE TOPPING
¼ cup packed brown sugar
Pinch of salt
⅔ cup coarsely chopped pecans

FOR THE CRUST
1 cup pecans, ground
1 cup graham cracker crumbs (nine
    2½" x 5" graham crackers, crushed)
3 tablespoons granulated sugar
6 tablespoons (¾ stick) unsalted
    butter, melted

FOR THE FILLING
3 (8-ounce) packages cream cheese,
    softened to room temperature
1 cup granulated sugar
¼ teaspoon salt
1 cup canned pumpkin
½ teaspoon ground cinnamon
½ teaspoon ground allspice
3 eggs
¼ cup heavy cream

PREPARE THE PRALINE TOPPING

Position a rack in the center of the oven and preheat the oven to 350°F. Line a baking sheet with foil and lightly grease it.

In a heavy medium saucepan, stir the sugar and salt over medium heat until the sugar melts and the mixture comes to a boil. Boil 1 minute without stirring. Mix in the pecans and remove from the heat. Spread the mixture onto the prepared baking sheet. Bake for 8 minutes, or until the mixture bubbles vigorously. Remove from the oven and allow the praline to cool completely on the baking sheet. Break the praline into ½" pieces and set aside. (This can be done 1 day ahead.) Store in an airtight container.

PREPARE THE CRUST

In a bowl, mix the pecans, graham cracker crumbs, sugar, and butter until the crumbs are evenly moistened. Press the mixture onto the bottom and two-thirds of the way up the sides of a 10" round springform pan. Bake for 10 minutes at 350°F. Remove from the oven and let cool. Reduce the oven temperature to 325°F.

PREPARE THE FILLING AND ASSEMBLE THE CHEESECAKE

In the bowl of an electric mixer, beat the cream cheese on medium speed until fluffy. Gradually add the sugar and salt, beating until combined. Add the pumpkin, cinnamon, and allspice, beating until well blended. Add the eggs, one at a time, beating well after each addition. Add the cream and beat until the mixture is completely blended. Pour the mixture into the cooled crust.

Place the springform pan in a roasting pan filled with enough hot water to come halfway up the sides of the springform pan. Bake for 1½ hours, or until the filling is puffy and golden on top but still jiggles slightly when gently shaken. Remove the springform pan from the water and set it on a wire rack to cool for at least 1 hour. Refrigerate at least 6 hours before serving.

Let the cake stand at room temperature for 20 minutes before serving. The cake will keep, covered and refrigerated, for up to 3 days.

Just before serving, evenly scatter the reserved praline pieces over the top of the cake.

Raspberry Ginger Cheesecake

Makes one 9" cake, 10–12 servings

With a little extra sweetness from the berries and a little extra kick from the ginger in both the cookie crust and the creamy filling, this cake is for cheesecake lovers who are ready to try something a little different. The tart red raspberries hidden in the center are a contrast in color, flavor, and texture.

FOR THE CRUST

2 cups graham cracker crumbs (eighteen 2½" x 5" graham crackers, crushed)

¼ cup sugar

1 teaspoon ground ginger

½ cup (1 stick) unsalted butter, melted

FOR THE FILLING

2 (8-ounce) packages cream cheese, softened

1 teaspoon freshly grated lemon zest

1 teaspoon very finely minced fresh ginger

¾ cup sugar

2 eggs

⅓ cup heavy cream

2 teaspoons pure vanilla extract

2 (6-ounce) baskets fresh red raspberries (about 2 cups)

2 teaspoons cornstarch

PREPARE THE CRUST

Position a rack in the center of the oven and preheat the oven to 350°F.

In a bowl, mix the graham cracker crumbs, sugar, ginger, and butter until the crumbs are evenly moistened. Press the mixture onto the bottom and two-thirds of the way up the sides of a 9" round springform pan. Bake 10 minutes. Remove the pan from the oven and set it aside to cool on a wire rack.

PREPARE THE FILLING AND ASSEMBLE THE CHEESECAKE

In the bowl of an electric mixer set on medium speed, beat the cream cheese, lemon zest, and ginger until fluffy. Gradually beat in the sugar. Add the eggs, one at a time, beating well after each addition. Beat in the cream and vanilla.

Pour two-thirds of the batter into the prepared crust. Place the pan in the freezer for 10 minutes.

In a medium bowl, toss the raspberries with the cornstarch until coated. Remove the pan from the freezer and sprinkle the berry mixture over the chilled filling. Pour the remaining filling over the berries to cover.

Place the springform pan in a roasting pan filled with enough hot water to come halfway up the sides of the springform pan. Bake for 1¼ hours, or until the filling is puffy and golden on top but still jiggles slightly when gently shaken. Remove the springform pan from the water and set on a wire rack to cool for at least 1 hour. Refrigerate the cake for at least 6 hours.

Let the cake stand at room temperature for 20 minutes before serving. When ready to serve, run a thin knife around the edges to loosen. Release and remove the pan sides.

The cake will keep, covered and refrigerated, for up to 3 days.

Serving suggestion: Serve slices garnished with a few fresh raspberries and mint leaves.

Lemon Mousse Cake

Makes one 8″ layer cake, 8–10 servings

A classic Greyston recipe, this cake has perfectly sweetened lemon flavors accenting a simple vanilla chiffon layer cake.

FOR THE LEMON CURD

2 large eggs
1 egg yolk
½ cup granulated sugar
⅓ cup fresh lemon juice (from about
   2 medium lemons)
⅛ teaspoon salt
¼ cup (½ stick) unsalted butter, cut
   into small pieces
1 teaspoon finely grated fresh
   lemon zest

FOR THE LEMON MOUSSE

1 cup heavy cream
¾ cup lemon curd

FOR THE LEMON BUTTERCREAM FROSTING

6 tablespoons (¾ stick) unsalted
   butter, softened to room
   temperature
2 cups confectioners' sugar, sifted
3 tablespoons heavy cream
1¼ teaspoons pure vanilla extract
1 teaspoon lemon extract

FOR THE CAKE

1 recipe Vanilla Chiffon Cake Layers
   (see page 16), baked and cooled
½ fresh lemon, seeds discarded

PREPARE THE LEMON CURD

In a small saucepan set over medium-low heat, whisk the eggs and egg yolk with the sugar, lemon juice, and salt. Continue to cook, whisking constantly, for 10 minutes, or until thickened. Remove the curd from the heat and add the butter, stirring until melted. Strain the mixture through a mesh sieve into a small bowl. Stir in the lemon zest. Cover with plastic wrap, pressing the plastic directly on the entire surface of the lemon curd to prevent a skin from forming. Chill the curd in the refrigerator until firm. (The curd can be made up to 1 week ahead.)

PREPARE THE LEMON MOUSSE

In the bowl of an electric mixer set on medium-high speed, beat the cream until it holds soft peaks. Working in three batches, gently fold the cream into the lemon curd. Refrigerate for at least 1 hour before using.

PREPARE THE LEMON BUTTERCREAM FROSTING

In a clean bowl of an electric mixer, combine the butter, sugar, cream, vanilla, and lemon extract. Mix on medium-low speed until well combined.

ASSEMBLE THE CAKE

With a long serrated knife, trim the rounded top off each cake layer to create a flat surface (see Toasted Crumb Garnish, page 33).

Squeeze half of the juice from the lemon over the cut side of one layer of cake. Place that layer, cut side up, on a serving plate. Spread the lemon mousse evenly on top.

Carefully place the next layer, cut side down, on top of the first layer. Squeeze the rest of the juice from the lemon on top. Frost the top and sides of the cake with the lemon buttercream frosting. Place the cake in the refrigerator for at least 1 hour to set. Keep refrigerated until ready to serve.

Serving suggestion: Press halved and thinly sliced lemons around the base of the cake, or top with Candied Citrus Strips (see page 29) or Candied Citrus Slices (see page 30) made with lemons.

Flourless Citrus Cake

Makes one 10" cake, about 12 servings

Winter is the best time to make this cake. The variety of citrus fruit is great, and the flavors are bright and pungent. Buy a variety of oranges to taste before deciding which to buy for the cake; it will pay off when you select the sweetest and most flavorful.

3 small unpeeled whole oranges
(Valencia or blood oranges work
best)
2 cups almond flour or ground
blanched almonds
1½ cups sugar

1 teaspoon baking powder
¼ teaspoon salt
5 eggs, separated
1 tablespoon freshly grated lemon zest
1 teaspoon pure vanilla extract

Put the oranges in a deep pot and add enough water to cover. (The oranges will float.) Bring the water to a boil, then lower to a simmer and cook, uncovered, for 1 hour, replenishing the water as it evaporates. Drain the oranges and set them aside until they are cool enough to handle. Cut each orange into eighths and remove the seeds.

Working in two batches, place the oranges in a food processor and process until they are finely chopped, or finely chop by hand. (You should have about 2 cups of chopped oranges when finished.) Set aside.

Position a rack in the center of the oven and preheat the oven to 375°F. Butter an 8" round springform pan and line the pan bottom with a parchment paper round. Set aside.

In a medium bowl, mix the flour or ground almonds with ¾ cup of the sugar, the baking powder, and salt. Set aside.

In a large bowl, whisk the egg yolks with ½ cup plus 2 tablespoons of the sugar until the eggs are thick and pale yellow in color. Stir in the lemon zest and vanilla. Continue to whisk for 5 minutes, or until thick. Fold in half of the reserved oranges and then half of the dry ingredients. Repeat with the remaining oranges and dry ingredients.

In a clean dry bowl, using clean dry beaters, beat the egg whites until they hold soft peaks. Gradually add the remaining 2 tablespoons of sugar, beating until the whites are stiff but not dry. Fold the whites into the orange batter in three additions, blending completely each time.

Pour the batter into the prepared pan and bake for 45 to 55 minutes, or until a wooden skewer inserted near the center comes out clean. (If the cake top browns too quickly, cover with foil.)

Set the pan on a wire rack and allow it to cool completely. Run a thin knife around the cake, and release and remove the sides of the pan. Transfer the cake to a serving plate.

This cake can be made 1 day ahead. Store at room temperature, wrapped in foil.

Serving suggestion: *Serve with vanilla ice cream or a citrus-flavored sherbet or sorbet.*

Grapefruit Yogurt Cake

Makes one 10" cake, about 12 servings

When making this cake, whole milk yogurt is the best choice. While pink grape-fruits are not necessary, they add a nice color. A Swiss yogurt company called Emmi makes a pink grapefruit yogurt; if this product is available in your area, you can substitute 1¼ cups of it for the yogurt in the recipe, reduce the juice to ¼ cup, and still add the zest.

2 cups unbleached all-purpose flour
1 tablespoon baking powder
¼ teaspoon salt
2 eggs
¾ cup granulated sugar
1 cup plain whole milk yogurt

⅓ cup vegetable oil
Juice (about ½ cup) and zest (about 1 tablespoon) of 1 pink grapefruit
1 teaspoon pure vanilla extract
3 tablespoons confectioners' sugar

Position a rack in the center of the oven and preheat the oven to 350°F. Grease a 10" round springform pan and line the pan bottom with a parchment paper round. Set aside.

In a medium bowl, whisk together the flour, baking powder, and salt to blend.

In a large bowl, beat the eggs and granulated sugar until the eggs are thick and pale yellow. Add the yogurt, oil, 1 tablespoon of the grapefruit juice, the grape-fruit zest, and vanilla. Stir well to combine. Add the flour mixture and stir to combine.

Pour the batter into the prepared pan, smoothing the top with a rubber spatula. Bake for 30 to 40 minutes, or until the top is golden brown and a wooden skewer comes out clean when inserted near the center. Place the pan on a wire rack for 10 minutes to cool. Run a thin knife around the edge of the pan to loosen the cake. Release and remove the pan sides. Cool completely on the wire rack.

In a small saucepan, combine the confectioners' sugar and the remaining grapefruit juice and bring to a boil. Reduce the heat to a simmer and cook, stirring, for 10 minutes, or until the glaze is slightly thickened. Remove from the heat.

To finish the cake, invert the cooled cake and remove the pan bottom. Carefully peel away the parchment. Reinvert the cake onto a serving plate. Pierce the cake all over the top with a skewer and pour the warm grapefruit syrup over it.

Serving suggestion: Make a border around the top and bottom edges with Candied Citrus Strips made with grapefruit (see page 29).

Orange Poppy Seed Cake

Makes one 10" cake, 10–12 servings

This one-layer cake is delicious served after lunch or a light summer dinner. It's especially good with Spiked Whipped Cream made with Grand Marnier (see page 27) or fresh seasonal berries.

FOR THE CAKE

1½ cups unbleached all-purpose flour, sifted
3 tablespoons poppy seeds
1 teaspoon baking powder
¼ teaspoon baking soda
¼ teaspoon salt
1 cup sugar
¾ cup (1½ sticks) unsalted butter, softened to room temperature
2 tablespoons freshly grated orange zest

4 eggs
½ cup milk
2 tablespoons freshly squeezed orange juice
1 teaspoon pure vanilla extract

FOR THE SYRUP

½ cup freshly squeezed orange juice
¼ cup Grand Marnier or other orange-flavored liqueur
3 tablespoons sugar

PREPARE THE CAKE

Position a rack in the center of the oven and preheat the oven to 350°F. Grease and flour a 10" round springform pan and line the pan bottom with a parchment paper round. Set aside.

In a bowl, whisk together the flour, poppy seeds, baking powder, baking soda, and salt to blend well. Set aside.

In the bowl of an electric mixer set on medium speed, cream the sugar, butter, and orange zest until the mixture becomes light and fluffy.

In a small bowl, lightly whisk together the eggs, milk, orange juice, and vanilla until the mixture is well combined. With the mixer set on low speed, slowly beat the egg mixture into the butter mixture. Add the dry ingredients in three batches, beating well after each addition.

Pour the batter into the prepared pan, smoothing the top with a rubber spatula. Bake for 30 to 40 minutes, or until a wooden skewer inserted near the center comes out clean and the top springs back when lightly touched. Remove the pan from the oven and set it on a wire rack to cool for 10 to 15 minutes, or until warm.

PREPARE THE SYRUP

In a small saucepan, combine the juice, liqueur, and sugar. Stir over medium heat until the sugar is completely dissolved. Reduce the heat to low and simmer 10 to 12 minutes longer, or until the syrup begins to thicken. Remove from the heat and set aside.

FINISH THE CAKE

While still in the pan, pierce the top of the cake all over with a thin skewer. Run a thin knife around the edges of the pan. Brush the top of the warm cake with several spoonfuls of the syrup, letting some of it run down between the cake and the side of the pan. Let the cake stand for 10 minutes.

Release and remove the sides of the pan, and carefully invert the cake onto the rack. Pierce the cake bottom all over with the skewer and spoon the remaining syrup over the bottom of the cake. Reinvert the cake onto the rack and let it cool completely.

Serving suggestion: *Serve with Spiked Whipped Cream made with Grand Marnier (see page 27) and fresh seasonal berries. Garnish with curls of orange peel.*

Anise Seed Cake
with Orange Icing

Makes one 8" cake, 8–10 servings

This cake makes a great birthday cake for someone who prefers something lighter and more complex in flavor than a traditional vanilla or chocolate layer cake.

FOR THE CAKE

2 cups unbleached all-purpose flour

1 tablespoon baking powder

½ cup (1 stick) unsalted butter,
    softened to room temperature

⅔ cup granulated sugar

1 tablespoon whole anise seeds,
    crushed

2 teaspoons freshly grated orange zest

3 eggs, separated

½ cup milk

½ cup freshly squeezed orange juice

½ teaspoon salt

¼ cup Apricot Glaze (see page 22)

FOR THE ICING

1 (8-ounce) package cream cheese,
    softened to room temperature

½ cup (1 stick) unsalted butter,
    softened to room temperature

3 cups confectioners' sugar, sifted

2 tablespoons orange-flavored liqueur
    such as Cointreau or Triple Sec

2 teaspoons freshly grated orange zest

PREPARE THE CAKE

Position a rack in the center of the oven and preheat the oven to 350°F. Grease and flour an 8" round springform pan and line the pan bottom with a parchment paper round.

In a small bowl, whisk together the flour and baking powder. Set aside.

In a large mixing bowl, with a mixer set on medium speed, cream the butter, sugar, anise seeds, and orange zest until light and fluffy. Add the egg yolks and continue to beat until well combined. Reduce the mixer speed to low, and add the milk and orange juice, beating until just combined, scraping down the sides with a rubber spatula, if necessary. Add the dry ingredients, increasing the mixer to medium speed until the dry ingredients are completely moistened.

In a clean dry bowl, using clean dry beaters, beat the egg whites and the salt with an electric mixer on medium-high speed, until they hold stiff peaks.

Stir about one-third of the egg whites into the batter to lighten it. Carefully fold in the remaining whites, in two batches, to blend thoroughly.

Pour the batter into the prepared pan. Bake for 30 to 35 minutes, or until the cake springs back when touched lightly near the center and a wooden skewer inserted near the center comes out clean. Set the pan on a wire rack and allow the cake to cool completely.

PREPARE THE ICING

In the bowl of an electric mixer, beat the cream cheese and butter on medium speed until fluffy. Gradually beat in the sugar until blended. Add the liqueur and orange zest and continue beating until well blended. Cover and refrigerate for 30 minutes, or until the icing is firm enough to spread.

FINISH THE CAKE

Run a thin knife around the inside edge of the pan to loosen. Release and remove the sides of the pan and invert the cake onto a plate. Remove the pan bottom and carefully peel away the parchment. With a long serrated knife, slice the cake horizontally into 2 equal layers.

Brush the cut surface of each layer with the Apricot Glaze. Spread a thick layer of icing (about 1½ cups) over the glazed surface of one layer. Gently place the frosted, glazed layer on top of the other layer, with the frosted side down. Frost the top and sides of the cake with the remaining icing. Chill until the frosting is set.

Serving suggestion: Tuck orange leaves under the cake on the platter, and then add a few orange blossoms. Or press 8 to 10 halved thin slices of fresh orange around the sides of the cake.

Apple Torte

Makes one 9" cake, 10–12 servings

Different from a traditional torte, which is made with very little flour, this apple dessert is a nice departure from a pie, and it's more elegant than a crisp. The fruit, tossed in ground spices and sweetened with sugar and maple syrup, sits on a delicious cream cheese base. The relatively short baking time allows the apples to retain their shape and a firm-tender texture.

FOR THE CRUST

½ cup (1 stick) unsalted butter, softened to room temperature
⅓ cup sugar
¼ teaspoon pure vanilla extract
1 cup unbleached all-purpose flour
½ cup apricot jam

FOR THE FILLING

1 (8-ounce) package cream cheese, softened to room temperature

½ cup sugar
1 egg
¼ teaspoon pure vanilla extract

FOR THE TOPPING

4 cups peeled apple slices
¼ cup sugar
¼ cup pure maple syrup
½ teaspoon ground cinnamon
¼ teaspoon ground cardamom
½ cup slivered almonds

PREPARE THE CRUST

Position a rack in the center of the oven and preheat the oven to 400°F. Grease a 9" round springform pan.

In the bowl of an electric mixer, cream the butter, sugar, and vanilla on medium speed. Using a fork or your fingers, work in the flour until the mixture resembles coarse crumbs. Press the mixture onto the bottom and 1" up the sides of the prepared pan. Pierce the bottom several times with the tines of a fork. Chill at least 30 minutes.

Line the chilled shell with parchment and fill with pie weights. Bake for 12 minutes, or until the pastry is set and golden. Carefully remove the parchment and weights and continue to bake the shell for 5 minutes longer, or until golden. If the edges start to brown too quickly, cover with strips of foil or piecrust shields (see page 9). Cool on a wire rack.

When the pastry is cool, spread the apricot jam evenly over the bottom of the crust and set aside.

PREPARE THE FILLING

Using an electric mixer set on medium speed, beat the cream cheese with the sugar until light. Beat in the egg and vanilla. Spread the filling evenly over the prepared crust.

PREPARE THE TOPPING

In a large bowl, combine the apples with the sugar, maple syrup, cinnamon, and cardamom. Arrange the apples in concentric circles over the filling. Sprinkle with the almonds.

Bake for 10 minutes, then reduce the oven temperature to 350°F and bake an additional 30 minutes, or until the apples are tender. Cool on a wire rack at least 30 minutes. Release and remove the pan sides. Cool completely, then refrigerate until ready to serve.

Fresh Berry Layer Cake

Makes one 8" layer cake, 8–10 servings

Try making the simple syrup called for in this recipe with kirsch, a cherry liqueur, or framboise, a raspberry liqueur. If you prepare the cake layers ahead of time, this is an incredibly fast and easy cake to assemble.

FOR THE ICING
1½ cups heavy cream
1 teaspoon pure vanilla extract
½ cup confectioners' sugar, sifted
2 cups strawberries, hulled and thinly
   sliced
1 cup blueberries, halved

FOR THE CAKE
1 recipe Vanilla Chiffon Cake Layers
   (see page 16), baked and cooled
¼ cup Simple Syrup (see page 24)
6 whole strawberries, stems removed
   and halved lengthwise
¼ cup whole blueberries

PREPARE THE ICING

Chill the bowl and beaters of an electric mixer for at least 15 minutes in the refrigerator. With the mixer set on medium speed, beat the cream and vanilla in the chilled bowl just until the cream holds soft peaks. With the mixer running, gradually add the sugar and continue to beat until the mixture holds stiff peaks. Remove one-quarter of the cream mixture and place it in a separate bowl with the thinly sliced strawberries and halved blueberries, folding the fruit into the cream. Place the cream mixture and cream/fruit mixture in the refrigerator until ready to assemble the cake.

PREPARE THE CAKE

Trim the rounded tops from both Vanilla Chiffon Cake Layers using a long serrated knife to create flat layers (see Toasted Crumb Garnish, page 33). Evenly sprinkle about half of the Simple Syrup over each layer.

Place one cake layer, cut side up, on a serving plate. Spread the cream/fruit mixture evenly over the top to within $\frac{1}{2}$" of the edge. Gently place the second layer, cut side down, on top. Spread the top and sides of the cake with the remaining whipped cream. Garnish the top of the cake with the halved strawberries and whole blueberries. Refrigerate until ready to serve.

Blueberry Sour Cream Torte

Makes one 9" cake, 10–12 servings

In this recipe, tangy sour cream and sweet blueberries are combined to produce a lush dessert that presents beautifully with a scoop of ice cream or dollop of sweetened sour cream.

FOR THE CRUST
1½ cups unbleached all-purpose flour
½ cup sugar
½ cup ground almonds
1½ teaspoons baking powder
½ teaspoon salt
½ cup (1 stick) unsalted butter

FOR THE FILLING
4 cups fresh blueberries
½ cup sugar

1 teaspoon fresh lemon juice
Zest of 1 lemon
½ teaspoon ground cinnamon
¼ cup cornstarch

FOR THE TOPPING
2 egg yolks
2 cups sour cream
½ cup sugar
1 teaspoon pure vanilla extract

PREPARE THE CRUST

Position a rack in the center of the oven and preheat the oven to 400°F. Grease a 9" round springform pan and line the pan bottom with a parchment paper round. Set aside.

In a large bowl, combine the flour, sugar, almonds, baking powder, and salt. Using a pastry blender or two knives, cut the butter into the dry ingredients until it forms coarse crumbs. Press the mixture onto the bottom of the prepared pan. Bake for 10 to 15 minutes, until the crust is golden. Remove the pan from the oven and set it aside to cool on a wire rack. Reduce the oven temperature to 350°F.

PREPARE THE FILLING

In a medium saucepan, toss the blueberries with the sugar, lemon juice, lemon zest, cinnamon, and cornstarch. Cook over medium heat until the blueberries are bubbling and beginning to burst, about 3 to 5 minutes, stirring gently several times. Reduce the heat to low and simmer for 3 minutes. Set aside to cool slightly.

PREPARE THE TOPPING

In a medium bowl, combine the egg yolks, sour cream, sugar, and vanilla. Mix until well combined.

FINISH THE TORTE

Spoon the filling over the crust. Spoon the topping evenly over the filling and smooth with a rubber spatula.

Bake for 45 minutes, or until the topping browns and appears to have set. Set the pan on a wire rack until completely cool. Release and remove pan sides.

Serving suggestion: *Serve warm or at room temperature with vanilla ice cream or a small dollop of sour cream sweetened to taste with maple syrup.*

Country Pear Cake

Makes one 9" cake, 8 servings

Rozanne Gold, a Greyston board member and cookbook author, provided this recipe. As she says, it is truly a cake of simple pleasure—especially since it's made in one bowl. You may use a single variety of pear, such as Comice, or try a mixture including Anjou and Bartlett.

....

2 eggs
¼ cup milk
⅓ cup good-quality olive oil
1 tablespoon freshly grated lemon zest

⅔ cup + 1 tablespoon sugar
1½ cups self-rising flour
4 large ripe pears (about 2 pounds)

....

Position a rack in the center of the oven and preheat the oven to 375°F. Grease and flour a 9" round cake pan. Set aside.

In a large bowl, whisk together the eggs, milk, oil, and lemon zest until thoroughly blended. Beat in ⅔ cup of the sugar. Stir in the flour and mix until a smooth batter is formed.

Peel the pears using a small sharp knife or vegetable peeler. Cut the pears lengthwise into quarters. Cut away the tough cores and any seeds. Slice the pear quarters crosswise into ¼" slices. Add the pears to the batter and stir gently so they are completely incorporated into the batter.

Pour the batter into the prepared pan. Sprinkle the top of the cake with the 1 tablespoon of sugar. Bake for 50 minutes. Set the pan on a wire rack to cool. Serve the cake warm or at room temperature.

Serving suggestion: *Serve with vanilla ice cream and a drizzle of Caramel Sauce (see page 25).*

Chocolate Obsession Cake

Makes one 8" cake, 8–10 servings

This recipe comes from Greyston board member and cookbook author Rozanne Gold, who says that for die-hard chocolate lovers, this is one of the easiest cakes you'll ever make. A hint of freshly grated orange zest reverberates with each bite.

1 pound good-quality semisweet chocolate, finely chopped
10 tablespoons (1¼ sticks) unsalted butter, cut into small pieces

6 eggs
¼ teaspoon salt
Freshly grated zest of 1 small orange

Position a rack in the center of the oven and preheat the oven to 375°F. Grease an 8" round springform pan and line the pan bottom with a parchment paper round. Set aside.

In the top of a double boiler over simmering water, melt the chocolate and butter, stirring until smooth. Remove from the heat and set aside.

In the bowl of an electric mixer, beat the eggs and salt for 6 minutes, or until the eggs triple in volume. Fold in the chocolate mixture, stirring by hand until they are completely blended. Stir in the orange zest.

Pour the batter into the prepared pan. Bake for 20 minutes. (The center will still be a little soft.) Set the pan on a wire rack to cool for at least 30 minutes. Run a thin knife around the edge of the pan to loosen. Release and remove the pan sides, and refrigerate if not serving immediately. (The cake can be refrigerated for up to 2 days.) Return the cake to room temperature before serving.

Serving suggestion: Dust with confectioners' sugar (see page 13) and serve with either Spiked Whipped Cream (see page 27) made with orange-flavored liqueur or orange flower water, or a dollop of Whipped Cream (see page 26) sprinkled with freshly grated orange zest. Garnish each slice with a Chocolate Curl (see page 31).

Lotus in Mud Cake

Makes one 10" cake, about 16 slim servings

This is by far Greyston's most intense chocolate dessert. A dense chocolate base filled with ganache, it was originally sold with a single buttercream flower piped onto the top. This garnish is meant to signify the way a lotus flower can grow up through muddy waters, a nod to the bakery's Buddhist roots and a metaphor for the work Greyston is doing with the surrounding community.

FOR THE SHELL
1¾ cups chocolate wafer crumbs
   (about 32 wafers, crushed)
½ cup (1 stick) unsalted butter, melted

FOR THE FILLING
¼ cup (½ stick) unsalted butter
7 ounces good-quality bittersweet
   chocolate

3 whole eggs, separated
⅓ cup sugar
¼ cup heavy cream
1 teaspoon pure vanilla extract
2 egg whites
¼ teaspoon salt

PREPARE THE SHELL

Position a rack in the center of the oven and preheat the oven to 350°F.

In a bowl, stir together the wafer crumbs and butter and combine well. Pat the mixture onto the bottom and 1" up the sides of a 10" round springform pan. Chill for 30 minutes.

PREPARE THE FILLING

In the top of a double boiler or metal bowl set over simmering water, melt the butter and chocolate together, stirring until smooth. Remove the mixture from the heat and set aside to cool slightly.

In the bowl of an electric mixer set on medium speed, beat the egg yolks and sugar for 3 minutes, or until thick and pale yellow.

Reduce the mixer speed to low and gradually add the chocolate mixture to the egg yolks, beating to combine. Add the cream and vanilla and continue mixing for 3 minutes, or until well combined. Set aside.

In a medium bowl, whisk the 5 egg whites with the salt until they are frothy but not holding peaks. Pour the egg whites into the chocolate mixture and stir gently to combine.

Pour the batter into the prepared shell. (If there are a lot of air bubbles in the filling, gently tap the bottom of the filled pan against a countertop covered with a dish towel until some of the bubbles are released.) Bake for 30 minutes, or until the center is set.

Set the pan on a wire rack to cool completely. Release and remove the sides.

Serving suggestion: Garnish with a dollop of softly Whipped Cream (see page 26) and white or dark Chocolate Curls (see page 31).

Chocolate Banana Nut Cake

Makes one 10" cake, 10–12 servings

I've always loved frozen chocolate-dipped bananas covered in walnuts. Here's a cake version of that childhood delicacy. Kids love a slim slice after school with a tall glass of milk. For more mature palates, serve it with a dollop of Spiked Whipped Cream (see page 27) that's been made with banana liqueur or rum. (Photo page 74)

¾ cup (1½ sticks) unsalted butter
6 ounces semisweet chocolate, finely
    chopped
1½ cups unbleached all-purpose flour
1 cup sugar
½ cup ground walnuts
2 teaspoons baking powder
½ teaspoon baking soda

¼ teaspoon salt
⅔ cup buttermilk
1 tablespoon pure vanilla extract
2 cups lightly mashed (5–6 whole) very
    ripe bananas
3 eggs, lightly beaten
¾ cup chopped walnuts

Position a rack in the center of the oven and preheat the oven to 350°F. Grease a 10" round cake pan and line the pan bottom with a parchment paper round.

In a saucepan over low heat, melt the butter. Add the chocolate, stirring until completely melted and smooth. Remove the pan from the heat and allow to cool slightly, about 10 minutes.

Meanwhile, in a large bowl, whisk together the flour, sugar, ground walnuts, baking powder, baking soda, and salt to blend thoroughly. Stir in the buttermilk, vanilla, and banana just until combined. Set aside.

Add the eggs to the cooled chocolate mixture and stir until well combined. Stir the chocolate mixture into the banana mixture until well combined.

Pour the batter into the prepared pan. Bake for 25 minutes. Remove the pan from the oven and carefully sprinkle the chopped walnuts across the top of the cake. (The cake will still jiggle in the middle.) Return the cake to the oven and bake for 25 minutes longer, or until a wooden skewer inserted near the center comes out clean.

Cool the cake on a wire rack for 15 minutes, then remove the cake from the pan and allow it to cool completely on a wire rack.

Serving suggestion: *Serve the cake dusted with confectioners' sugar (see page 13) or topped with Spiked Whipped Cream (see page 27).*

German Chocolate Cake

Makes one 8" layer cake, 8–10 servings

German Chocolate Cake is not named, as is sometimes reported, for German immigrants who brought it to the United States. The cake actually takes its name from an American named Sam German, who created a mild dark baking chocolate bar for Baker's Chocolate Company in 1852. The chocolate bar, Baker's German's Sweet Chocolate, became associated with a recipe for a cake made with sweet milk, shredded coconut, and nuts. In most recipes, the apostrophe and the "s" have been dropped, giving a false sense of the cake's origins.

FOR THE ICING
1 (12-ounce) can evaporated milk
1¼ cups sugar
¾ cup (1½ sticks) unsalted butter,
    melted and cooled
5 egg yolks
1 teaspoon pure almond extract
¼ teaspoon salt
1 cup sweetened shredded coconut

½ cup sliced almonds, toasted
½ cup pecan pieces

FOR THE CAKE
1 recipe Chocolate Chiffon Cake
    Layers (see page 17), baked and
    cooled
¾ cup sweetened shredded coconut

PREPARE THE ICING

In the top of a double boiler set over simmering water, combine the evaporated milk, sugar, butter, egg yolks, almond extract, and salt. Cook, stirring constantly and maintaining a simmer for 10 minutes, or until the mixture is thick enough to coat the back of a wooden spoon.

Remove from the heat and add the coconut, almonds, and pecans. Cool for 20 minutes, or until the mixture is thick enough to spread over the cake but still slightly warm.

ASSEMBLE THE CAKE

With a long serrated knife, trim the rounded top off each cake layer to create a flat surface (see Toasted Crumb Garnish, page 33).

Place one cake layer, cut side up, on a serving plate. Evenly spread one-quarter of the icing over the top of the first layer. Stir the coconut into the remaining icing. Place the second layer on top of the first cake layer, cut side down. Evenly spread the remaining icing over the top and sides of the cake.

Chill the cake in the refrigerator for at least 2 hours, or until the icing is completely set.

Mexican Hot Chocolate Cake

Makes one 10" cake, about 12 servings

Mexican chocolate is made from dark, bitter chocolate mixed with sugar, cinnamon, and sometimes nuts. The end result is a somewhat "grainy" product. It is most often sold in disks under the label Ibarra or Abuelita. (If Mexican chocolate is unavailable, use bittersweet chocolate and add 1 teaspoon of cinnamon to the topping and another 2 teaspoons of cinnamon to the cake batter.) This cake is dense and also grainy, making it a very textural experience. The addition of chili powder is a wink to mole sauce, a traditional Mexican concoction that contains chocolate, nuts, and hot chilies.

FOR THE TOPPING
⅓ cup unbleached all-purpose flour
3 tablespoons packed brown sugar
3 tablespoons butter, softened to
 room temperature
1 disk (3.15 ounces) Mexican
 chocolate, finely chopped

FOR THE CAKE
1 cup almond flour, or 7 ounces finely
 ground blanched almonds

¾ cup unbleached all-purpose flour
½ teaspoon chili powder, preferably
 Ancho, or more to taste
½ teaspoon salt
½ cup (1 stick) unsalted butter
2 disks (6.3 ounces) Mexican
 chocolate, finely chopped
4 eggs, separated
¾ cup granulated sugar
½ cup buttermilk

PREPARE THE TOPPING

In a bowl, stir the flour and sugar together until well blended. Either rub the butter into the flour mixture with your fingers or cut it in with knives or a pastry blender until the mixture resembles coarse crumbs. Stir in the chocolate and set aside. (This topping may be made up to 1 week in advance and stored in an airtight container in the refrigerator.)

PREPARE THE CAKE

Position a rack in the center of the oven and preheat the oven to 350°F. Grease a 10" round springform pan and line the pan bottom with a parchment paper round. Set aside.

In a bowl, whisk together the almond flour (or almonds), all-purpose flour, chili powder, and salt until thoroughly combined. Set aside.

In a small saucepan set over medium-low heat, melt the butter. Add the chocolate and stir until completely melted. Set aside to cool slightly.

In a medium bowl, whisk the egg yolks and sugar until pale yellow. Gradually stir in the cooled chocolate mixture. Stir in half of the reserved dry ingredients, and then add the buttermilk and stir to combine. Add the remaining dry ingredients and blend thoroughly.

In a clean dry bowl, using clean dry beaters, beat the egg whites on medium-high speed until they hold stiff peaks. Stir about one-third of the beaten egg whites into the chocolate mixture to lighten. Carefully fold in the remaining whites, in two batches, until well blended. Pour the batter into the prepared pan.

Lightly and evenly sprinkle the reserved topping mixture over the cake batter. (It will sink into the cake as it bakes.) Bake for 45 minutes, or until the cake springs back when lightly touched in the center. Set the pan on a wire rack for 15 minutes to cool. Release and remove the pan sides. Cool the cake to lukewarm or room temperature. Invert the cake and remove the pan bottom, then carefully peel away the parchment. Reinvert and cut into wedges to serve.

Serving suggestion: Top each slice with Whipped Cream (see page 26) sprinkled with cinnamon.

Chocolate Molten Cakelets

Makes six single-serving cakes

These little cakes are astonishingly easy to make and are guaranteed to wow guests. The batter can be made ahead of time, and when the time comes for dessert, just pop them in the oven for a few minutes. Take care not to overcook them. For the tidiest presentation, run a sharp paring knife around the edge of the ramekin before removing them. Like pancakes, the first one often comes out a mess, but with practice you will get better at releasing the cakes.

10 ounces good-quality bittersweet or semisweet chocolate, chopped
¼ cup (½ stick) unsalted butter, softened to room temperature
½ cup sugar

3 eggs
1½ teaspoons brandy or pure vanilla extract
⅛ teaspoon salt
¼ cup unbleached all-purpose flour

Position a rack in the center of the oven and preheat the oven to 400°F. Grease six 6-ounce ramekins and line the bottoms with parchment paper rounds.

In the top of a double boiler set over simmering water, melt the chocolate. Stir until smooth and remove from the heat, allowing the chocolate to cool slightly.

In the bowl of an electric mixer, cream the butter with the sugar on medium speed. Add the eggs, brandy (or vanilla), and salt, beating until well combined. Sprinkle the flour over the batter and blend on low speed. Add the cooled chocolate and mix until well blended.

Divide the batter among the prepared ramekins and place them on a baking sheet. Bake the cakes for 10 to 12 minutes, or until the tops are puffed and dry and a wooden skewer inserted in the center comes out with some batter clinging to it. (Take care not to overcook the cakes.) Remove the cakes from the oven. Grasping each ramekin with a dry kitchen towel, run a sharp, thin paring knife around the edge of the ramekin to release. Turn each cake out onto a small plate or into a shallow bowl. Serve immediately.

Serving suggestion: Serve with ice cream, Whipped Cream (see page 26), or Crème Fraîche (see page 28) sprinkled with Chocolate Curls (see page 31).

Sugared Four-Berry Tart (see recipe, page 127)

CHOCOLATE BANANA NUT CAKE (SEE RECIPE, PAGES 66–67)

74

Steamed Lemon Cakelets (see recipe, pages 92–93)

Rhubarb Strawberry Tart (see recipe, page 129)

RED VELVET CUPCAKES (SEE RECIPE, PAGES 94–95)

CARROT CAKE (SEE RECIPE, PAGES 96–97)

Fresh Coconut Mousse Cake (see recipe, pages 98–99)

79

Triple Chocolate Mousse Cake

Makes one 8" layer cake, 8–10 servings

This cake has a smooth and rich mousse, sandwiched between three light and fluffy cake layers. With a deep chocolate glaze covering the entire cake, it's no surprise that Triple Chocolate Mousse Cake is one of the most popular desserts at the Greyston Bakery. (Photo page 152)

FOR THE CAKE
6 eggs, separated
¾ cup vegetable oil
½ cup milk
1½ teaspoons pure vanilla extract
1 cup unbleached all-purpose flour
1½ cups sugar
¾ cup unsweetened cocoa powder
2 teaspoons baking powder
1 teaspoon baking soda
⅛ teaspoon salt

FOR THE MOUSSE
⅔ cup unsweetened cocoa powder
½ cup sugar
2 cups heavy cream

FOR THE GLAZE
¾ cup water
¼ cup sugar
12 ounces semisweet chocolate, chopped
½ lightly beaten egg

PREPARE THE CAKE

Position a rack in the center of the oven and preheat the oven to 350°F. Grease and flour three 8" round cake pans and line the pan bottoms with parchment paper rounds.

In a small bowl, whisk together the egg yolks, oil, milk, and vanilla until well combined. Set aside.

In a large bowl, whisk together the flour, 1 cup of the sugar, the cocoa powder, baking powder, baking soda, and salt. Add the egg yolk mixture and stir to blend. Set aside.

continued on page 82

In a clean dry bowl, using clean dry beaters, beat the egg whites on medium speed until they hold soft peaks. Gradually beat in the remaining ½ cup sugar. Continue to beat until the whites form stiff peaks.

Stir about one-third of the egg whites into the batter to lighten. Gently fold in the remaining whites, in two batches, until completely blended.

Pour the batter into the prepared pans, filling them equally.

Bake the cake for 25 to 30 minutes, or until the sides of the cakes begin to pull away from the pans and a wooden skewer inserted near the center of the cake comes out clean.

Set the pans on wire racks and allow them to cool for 10 minutes. Turn the layers out and carefully peel away the parchment. Reinvert the cakes onto the racks to cool completely.

PREPARE THE MOUSSE

In a small bowl, whisk together the cocoa powder and sugar to blend. Set aside.

In the bowl of an electric mixer set on medium speed, beat the cream, slowly adding the cocoa mixture until the cream is softly whipped. Store in the refrigerator until you are ready to assemble the cake.

ASSEMBLE THE CAKE

Trim the rounded tops of the cake layers using a long serrated knife to create flat layers (see Toasted Crumb Garnish, page 33).

Place one cake layer on a serving plate, cut side up. Spread half of the mousse evenly over the top. Place the second layer on top of the first, cut side down. Spread the remaining mousse on top of the second layer, and place the third cake layer on top, cut side down. (The top cake layer will have no mousse on the top.) Chill for at least 1 hour.

In a medium saucepan over medium heat, bring $\frac{1}{4}$ cup of the water and the sugar to a simmer, stirring until the sugar dissolves. Stir in the remaining $\frac{1}{2}$ cup water and bring to a simmer. Add the chocolate and stir until completely melted. Remove the pan from the heat and allow the glaze to cool for 5 minutes. Gently stir in the egg. Allow the glaze to cool further until lukewarm.

Pour the warm glaze over the edges of the chilled cake, allowing it to spill over the sides, spreading and smoothing it with a spatula as you go. To glaze the top, slowly pour the glaze across the top of the cake, but do not spread, allowing it to settle into a smooth layer. Refrigerate at least 1 hour before serving.

Serving suggestion: Decorate the top with Chocolate Leaves (see page 32), and lightly press Toasted Crumb Garnish (see page 33) onto the side.

Mocha Kahlúa Cake

Makes one 8" layer cake, about 8 servings

This luscious cake is a great way to celebrate the birthday of a coffee-lover. Layers of silky dark chocolate cake are accented with rich Kahlúa custard and covered in a mocha frosting. Serve with a scoop of ice cream: vanilla for a simple creamy accompaniment or coffee and chocolate to revel in the cake's flavors.

FOR THE CAKE

¾ cup good-quality unsweetened
  dark cocoa powder
1 tablespoon instant espresso powder
¾ cup hot water
1½ cups granulated sugar
1 cup unbleached all-purpose flour
2 teaspoons baking powder
1 teaspoon baking soda
¼ teaspoon salt
6 eggs, separated
¾ cup vegetable oil
1½ teaspoons pure vanilla extract
2 egg whites (reserve yolks for
  custard)
3 tablespoons Kahlúa or other
  coffee-flavored liqueur

FOR THE KAHLÚA CUSTARD

⅓ cup granulated sugar
1 tablespoon cornstarch
1¼ cups half-and-half
2 egg yolks (reserved from cake
  ingredients), lightly beaten
2 tablespoons Kahlúa or other coffee-
  flavored liqueur

FOR THE MOCHA FROSTING

½ cup (1 stick) unsalted butter,
  softened to room temperature
¼ cup good-quality unsweetened dark
  cocoa powder
3 tablespoons Kahlúa or other coffee-
  flavored liqueur
3 cups confectioners' sugar, sifted
2 tablespoons half-and-half

PREPARE THE CAKE

Position a rack in the center of the oven and preheat the oven to 350°F. Butter and flour three 8" round cake pans and line the pan bottoms with parchment rounds. Set aside.

In a large metal bowl, combine the cocoa powder and espresso powder. Add the hot water and stir to blend. Set aside to cool.

In a separate bowl, whisk 1 cup of the sugar with the flour, baking powder, baking soda, and salt to blend.

Beat the 6 egg yolks, oil, and vanilla into the cocoa mixture, then stir in the dry ingredients.

In the bowl of an electric mixer, beat the 8 egg whites until soft peaks form. Gradually add the remaining ½ cup sugar and continue beating until the mixture holds stiff peaks.

Stir about one-third of the egg whites into the prepared batter to lighten. Carefully fold the remaining whites, in two batches, into the batter until thoroughly combined. Divide the batter equally among the prepared pans.

Bake for 25 minutes, or until the cake layers begin to pull away from the sides of the pans and a wooden skewer inserted near the center comes out clean. Set the pans on a wire rack for 10 minutes to cool. Turn the cake layers out of the pans and carefully peel away the parchment. Reinvert the cake layers onto the wire rack. While the layers are still warm, brush each with 1 tablespoon Kahlúa (or coffee-flavored liqueur). Cool completely.

PREPARE THE KAHLÚA CUSTARD

In a saucepan, mix the sugar and cornstarch. Gradually stir in the half-and-half and egg yolks. Cook, stirring constantly, over medium heat for 7 minutes, or until the custard thickens. Remove the custard from the heat and stir in the Kahlúa (or coffee-flavored liqueur). Chill at least 20 minutes, or until cooled.

PREPARE THE MOCHA FROSTING

In a mixing bowl, beat the butter with the cocoa powder and Kahlúa (or coffee-flavored liqueur). Gradually add the sugar, mixing until combined. Beat in the half-and-half.

FINISH THE CAKE

With a long serrated knife, trim the rounded top off each cake layer to create a flat surface (see Toasted Crumb Garnish, page 33).

continued on page 86

Place the first layer on a serving plate, cut side up. Spread half of the custard on top of the first layer, to within ½" of the edge. Place the second layer on top of the first layer, cut side down, and spread the top with the remaining custard. Top with the third layer, cut side down. Refrigerate the assembled cake at least 1 hour to allow the custard to become firm. Spread the frosting over the top and sides of the cake. Refrigerate until ready to serve.

Serving suggestion: *Serve with vanilla, chocolate, or coffee ice cream.*

Burnt Almond Torte

Makes one 8" torte, 8–10 servings

This recipe comes from a little restaurant in northern Spain where I had lunch as I was writing the book. The owners, a husband and wife, were interested in the story of Greyston and the book I was writing, so they offered the recipe for this torte. Onto a paper napkin in Spanish, they quickly scribbled the ingredients and vague instructions. I carried the napkin home and tested the recipe several times to get it right. The sliced almonds on the top of the torte should be a deep brown color when the cake is done. If they are still pale, run the torte very briefly under the broiler.

1 cup finely ground almonds or
    almond meal
¼ cup unbleached all-purpose flour
1 teaspoon baking powder
¼ teaspoon salt
¾ cup granulated sugar

4 whole eggs
3 egg yolks
2 tablespoons unsalted butter, melted
1 teaspoon pure almond extract
½ cup sliced almonds
1 tablespoon confectioners' sugar

Position a rack in the center of the oven and preheat the oven to 400°F. Grease and flour an 8" round springform pan and line the pan bottom with a parchment paper round.

In a small bowl, whisk together the ground almonds or almond meal, flour, baking powder, and salt to blend. Set aside.

With an electric mixer set on medium speed, combine the granulated sugar, whole eggs, egg yolks, butter, and almond extract. Beat on medium speed for 1 minute, or until mixed very well. With a wooden spoon, gradually stir in the dry ingredients, blending well.

Pour the mixture into the prepared pan, sprinkle with the sliced almonds, and bake for 20 minutes, or until a wooden skewer inserted near the center comes out almost clean. Cool on a wire rack. Release and remove the sides of the pan. Dust with the confectioners' sugar before serving.

After-Dinner Mint Torte

Makes one 8" cake, 10–12 servings

This is an appropriately rich and sophisticated finish to an elegant meal. With a thin layer of minty white chocolate, this is reminiscent of intermission treats at the opera and mints slipped onto your pillow at the finest hotels.

FOR THE GANACHE
¾ cup heavy cream
6 ounces semisweet or bittersweet chocolate, finely chopped

FOR THE TORTE
7 ounces good-quality semisweet or bittersweet chocolate, chopped
¾ cup (1½ sticks) unsalted butter, softened to room temperature
1 teaspoon mint extract
¼ cup chopped blanched almonds
3 tablespoons unbleached all-purpose flour

2 tablespoons unsweetened cocoa powder
4 eggs, separated, at room temperature
⅔ cup sugar
⅛ teaspoon salt

FOR THE FILLING
6 ounces white chocolate, chopped
3 tablespoons heavy cream
1 teaspoon mint extract

PREPARE THE GANACHE

In a medium saucepan, bring the cream to a simmer over medium-high heat. Remove from the heat and whisk in the chocolate until it is completely melted and smooth. Transfer the ganache to a bowl and chill, covered, for 4 hours. Stir the ganache occasionally, until it is thick but still spreadable.

PREPARE THE TORTE

Position a rack in the center of the oven and preheat the oven to 350°F. Grease an 8" round springform pan and line the pan bottom with a parchment paper round.

In the top of a double boiler, melt the chocolate and butter together. Stir until smooth and remove from the heat. (Alternatively, in a microwaveable bowl, melt the chocolate and butter together in a microwave oven on medium power, checking and stirring after 2 minutes, and then checking and stirring every 30 seconds, until completely melted.) Stir in the mint extract. Set aside.

In a food processor, combine the almonds, flour, and cocoa powder and pulse several times until the mixture is like a coarse meal. Set aside.

In a separate bowl, whisk the egg yolks with ⅓ cup of the sugar until they are thick and pale yellow in color. Gradually stir in the melted chocolate mixture.

In a clean dry mixing bowl, with clean dry beaters, beat the egg whites with the salt until they hold soft peaks. Slowly add the remaining ⅓ cup sugar and beat until they hold stiff, glossy peaks.

Fold the almond mixture and about one-third of the egg whites into the chocolate batter until well combined. Carefully fold in one-half of the remaining egg whites, until completely blended. Repeat with the remaining whites. Pour the batter into the prepared pan. Bake for 35 to 45 minutes, or until a wooden skewer inserted near the center comes out clean. Set the pan on a wire rack and allow to cool completely.

PREPARE THE FILLING

In a skillet, bring about 1" of water to a boil. Remove from the heat. In a heat-proof bowl, combine the chocolate and the cream. Set the bowl in the hot water until the chocolate is melted, stirring a few times. (Alternatively, in a microwaveable bowl, melt the chocolate and cream together in a microwave oven with the power set at low for 2 to 2½ minutes.) Ensure that all of the chocolate melts, but do not overheat, as white chocolate burns very easily. The mixture may appear translucent while hot. Stir in the mint extract. Set aside to cool slightly.

continued on page 90

FINISH THE TORTE

Run a thin knife around the inside edge of the springform pan to loosen. Release and remove the sides of the pan and invert the cake onto a plate. Remove the pan bottom and carefully peel away the parchment. With a long serrated knife, slice the cake horizontally into two equal layers. Spread the filling evenly over the top of one layer to within ½" of the edge and carefully place the second layer on top. Chill the torte in the freezer for 30 minutes, or in the refrigerator for at least 1 hour.

Before frosting the torte, ensure the ganache has reached spreading consistency. Evenly spread all but about ¼ cup of the ganache over the top and sides of the torte. Chill the torte for about 1 hour, or until the ganache is firm. If necessary, use the reserved ganache to seal in any loose crumbs or to repair any bald spots. Rechill if the ganache has softened.

Serving suggestion: Decorate with a dusting of confectioners' sugar (see page 13), and garnish with Chocolate Leaves made from mint leaves (see page 32) or sprigs of fresh mint.

Olive Oil and Sherry Soufflé Cake
Makes 1 Bundt cake, 8–10 servings

This recipe is based on a traditional Italian dessert. Because of the egg whites whipped into the batter, it comes out incredibly light and spongy. If you do not have sherry, substitute a white wine on the sweeter side, such as Muscat or sauterne. For the best flavor, use fresh extra-virgin olive oil. (Photo page 150)

5 eggs, separated
¾ cup granulated sugar
1 tablespoon freshly grated lemon zest
1 tablespoon chopped rosemary
½ cup dry sherry

⅓ cup extra-virgin olive oil
1 cup unbleached all-purpose flour
½ teaspoon salt
3 tablespoons confectioners' sugar

Position a rack in the center of the oven and preheat the oven to 325°F. Grease and flour a 10" x 4½" tube cake pan or a 12-cup Bundt pan. Set aside.

In a medium bowl, whisk the egg yolks with the granulated sugar until the yolks are thick and pale yellow. Stir in the lemon zest and rosemary. Whisk in the sherry and oil. Gradually stir in the flour until well combined.

In a clean dry bowl, using clean dry beaters, beat the egg whites and salt until the whites hold firm peaks. Gently stir about one-third of the whites into the batter to lighten. Fold the remaining whites into the batter in two batches, blending completely.

Pour the batter into the prepared pan and smooth out the top with a rubber spatula. Bake for 40 minutes, or until the cake is deep golden brown and a wooden skewer inserted halfway between the outer and inner edges of the pan comes out clean. Set the pan on a wire rack to cool completely.

Remove the cake from the pan and transfer to a serving platter. Dust with the confectioners' sugar.

Serving suggestion: *Instead of the confectioners' sugar, serve slices with Créme Fraîche (see page 28) sprinkled with grated orange zest.*

Steamed Lemon Cakelets

Makes 6 single-serving cakes

Very easy to prepare, these little cakes have a light cake bottom and a rich pudding top. Based on traditional Pudding Cakes, the proportion of dry to wet ingredients is out of balance, causing the cake to separate into the two layers. They are best eaten warm, straight from the oven. (Photo page 75)

....

¾ cup sugar
⅓ cup unbleached all-purpose flour
3 eggs, separated
2 tablespoons butter, softened to
    room temperature

1 cup milk
5 tablespoons fresh lemon juice
1 teaspoon finely grated lemon zest
¼ teaspoon salt

....

Place a rack in the center of the oven and preheat the oven to 350°F. Grease six 6-ounce ramekins and set in a baking dish large enough to accommodate the ramekins with space in between.

In a medium bowl, whisk together the sugar and flour to blend. Set aside.

In the bowl of an electric mixer set on low speed, beat the egg yolks and butter until blended. Add the milk, lemon juice, and lemon zest, and beat for a few seconds until well combined. Pour the mixture over the dry ingredients and stir gently with a rubber spatula, breaking up any lumps.

In a clean dry bowl, with clean dry beaters, beat the egg whites with the salt on medium-high speed, until they hold stiff peaks. Carefully fold the egg whites into the batter and divide the batter evenly between the ramekins.

Pour very hot water in the baking dish until it comes halfway up the sides of the ramekins. (Take care not to splash water onto the batter.)

Bake for 30 to 35 minutes, or until the cakes are puffy and the tops are light golden brown.

Carefully transfer the ramekins to a wire rack to cool for 20 minutes. Run a small thin knife around the edges, then invert onto small plates and serve warm, or refrigerate and serve chilled.

The cakelets can be kept in the refrigerator, covered, for up to 3 days.

Serving suggestion: *Serve with a small dollop of Whipped Cream (see page 26) or dusted with confectioners' sugar (see page 13).*

Red Velvet Cupcakes

Makes 12 cupcakes

A fun way to serve these cupcakes is to peel the paper liners away from the cupcakes and slice them in half horizontally. Spread frosting over the top of the bottom halves, cover with the tops, and frost the tops; you'll have a festive handheld layer cake. (Photo page 77)

FOR THE CUPCAKES

2¼ cups unbleached all-purpose flour
1⅓ cups granulated sugar
1 teaspoon baking soda
1 teaspoon salt
¼ cup unsweetened cocoa powder
2 eggs
1 cup buttermilk
1 teaspoon distilled white vinegar
1 cup vegetable oil
2 tablespoons (1 ounce) red food coloring
1 teaspoon pure vanilla extract

FOR THE FROSTING

1 (8-ounce) package cream cheese, softened to room temperature
½ cup (1 stick) unsalted butter, softened to room temperature
4 cups (about a 1-pound package) confectioners' sugar, sifted
2 teaspoons pure vanilla extract

PREPARE THE CUPCAKES

Position a rack in the center of the oven and preheat the oven to 350°F. Line a 12-cup muffin tin with paper liners and set aside.

In a bowl, whisk together the flour, sugar, baking soda, salt, and cocoa powder to blend. Set aside.

In the bowl of an electric mixer set on medium speed, lightly beat the eggs. Add the buttermilk, vinegar, oil, food coloring, and vanilla, beating until well combined. Slowly add the dry ingredients, mixing until combined.

Pour the batter into the prepared muffin cups, filling each cup about two-thirds full. Bake for 25 to 35 minutes, or until a wooden skewer inserted near the center of a cupcake comes out clean. Remove the tin from the oven and cool on a wire rack for 10 minutes. Turn the cupcakes out of the tin and place them on the wire rack to cool completely.

PREPARE THE FROSTING

In the bowl of an electric mixer set on medium-high speed, cream the cream cheese and butter. Reduce the speed to low and gradually beat in the confectioners' sugar, until the mixture is fluffy. Beat in the vanilla.

Spread a few spoonfuls of frosting on top of each completely cooled cupcake.

Carrot Cake

Makes one 8" layer cake, 8–10 servings

Here is a Greyston classic: two layers of moist spice cake baked with fresh carrots, raisins, and walnuts. Inside and out, this cake has natural cream cheese filling and icing. As a finishing touch, the edges of the cake are dusted with chopped walnuts. (Photo page 78)

FOR THE CAKE

2 cups unbleached all-purpose flour
1½ teaspoons ground cinnamon
1½ teaspoons baking soda
1 teaspoon baking powder
½ teaspoon freshly grated nutmeg
½ teaspoon salt
2 cups packed brown sugar
½ cup (1 stick) unsalted butter, melted and cooled to room temperature
½ cup buttermilk
3 eggs
2 teaspoons pure vanilla extract
2 cups finely grated carrots (about ½ pound)
½ cup raisins
½ cup chopped walnuts

FOR THE FROSTING

12 ounces cream cheese (1½ 8-ounce packages), softened to room temperature
6 tablespoons (¾ stick) unsalted butter, softened to room temperature
1 tablespoon pure vanilla extract
2 cups confectioners' sugar, sifted
1 teaspoon grated orange zest
1 cup finely chopped walnuts

PREPARE THE CAKE

Position a rack in the center of the oven and preheat the oven to 350°F. Grease and flour two 8" round cake pans and line the pan bottoms with parchment paper rounds. Set aside.

In a large bowl, whisk together the flour, cinnamon, baking soda, baking powder, nutmeg, and salt to blend. Set aside.

In the bowl of an electric mixer set on medium speed (or by hand), combine the sugar, butter, buttermilk, eggs, and vanilla. Beat until light and fluffy.

Reduce the mixer speed to low and gradually add the dry ingredients. Continue to mix until combined. With a spoon, stir in the carrots, raisins, and walnuts.

Divide the batter evenly between the prepared pans. Bake for 30 to 40 minutes, or until the sides of the cakes begin to pull away from the pans and a wooden skewer inserted in the center comes out clean.

Set the pans on a wire rack to cool for 10 minutes. Turn the cakes out and carefully peel away the parchment. Reinvert onto the rack and cool completely.

PREPARE THE FROSTING

In the bowl of an electric mixer, beat the cream cheese with the butter and vanilla on high speed until smooth. Reduce the speed to low and gradually beat in the sugar. Stir in the orange zest. Chill at least 1 hour before using.

Spread the frosting on top of one cake layer. Carefully set the second layer on top. Spread the remaining frosting over the top and sides of the cake. Carefully press the handfuls of chopped walnuts onto the sides of the cake.

Fresh Coconut Mousse Cake

Makes one 8" layer cake, 8–10 servings

This coconut cake uses fresh coconut instead of the sweetened coconut traditionally used in baking. It makes for a subtler and more natural flavor. (Photo page 79)

FOR THE CAKE

1½ cups unbleached all-purpose flour
2½ teaspoons baking powder
¼ teaspoon salt
5 eggs, separated
1¼ cups granulated sugar
¼ cup (½ stick) unsalted butter, melted and cooled
½ cup milk

1 teaspoon pure vanilla extract
2 teaspoons pure coconut extract

FOR THE COCONUT MOUSSE

3 cups heavy cream
½ cup confectioners' sugar, sifted
1 teaspoon pure vanilla extract
¾ teaspoon pure coconut extract
3 cups shredded fresh coconut (from 2 coconuts)

PREPARE THE CAKE

Position a rack in the center of the oven and preheat the oven to 350°F. Grease and flour three 8" round cake pans. Line the pan bottoms with parchment paper rounds and set aside.

In a small bowl, whisk together the flour, baking powder, and salt to blend well.

In the bowl of an electric mixer set on medium speed, beat the egg yolks with 1 cup of the sugar until they are thick and pale yellow in color. Add the butter, milk, vanilla, and coconut extract and beat to combine well. With the mixer set on low speed, gradually add the dry ingredients. Set aside.

In a clean dry bowl, using clean dry beaters, beat the egg whites on medium-high speed, until they hold soft peaks. Reduce the mixer speed to medium and gradually add the remaining ¼ cup sugar, beating until the whites hold stiff peaks. Gently fold the egg whites into the batter, in two batches, to blend thoroughly.

Divide the batter equally in the prepared pans. Bake for 30 to 35 minutes, or until the cakes begin to pull away from the sides of the pans and a wooden skewer inserted near the center of the cake comes out clean. Set the pans on a wire rack and let cool for 10 minutes. Turn the cakes out and carefully peel away the parchment. Reinvert onto the wire rack and let cool completely.

PREPARE THE COCONUT MOUSSE

In the bowl of an electric mixer, beat the cream and sugar on medium-high speed for 3 to 5 minutes, or until soft peaks are formed.

Add the vanilla and coconut extract and beat 1 minute longer. Fold in 1 cup of the coconut. Chill for at least 1 hour.

ASSEMBLE THE CAKE

With a serrated bread knife, trim the rounded top of each layer to create a flat surface (see Toasted Crumb Garnish, page 33).

Place one layer, cut side up, on a serving plate. Evenly spread 1 cup of the coconut mousse on the top of the first layer. Gently place the second layer, cut side down, on top of the first layer. Spread 1 cup of the coconut mousse on the top of the second layer and place the third cake layer on top, cut side down.

Spread the top and sides of the cake with the remaining coconut mousse. Carefully pat handfuls of the remaining 2 cups coconut around the sides and top of the cake. Refrigerate at least 1 hour before serving.

Serving suggestion: *Place a few hibiscus, orchid, or other tropical flowers around the base of the cake.*

Grand Marnier Soufflé Cake

Makes one 8" cake, 8–10 servings

Flourless, quick, and easy, this cake is hard to resist when you have guests coming for dinner. If you make it ahead of time, it can be covered in plastic wrap and stored for 1 day.

8 ounces good-quality semisweet or
    bittersweet chocolate
½ cup (1 stick) unsalted butter
¼ cup strong espresso
2 tablespoons Grand Marnier,
    Cointreau, or other orange-
    flavored liqueur

6 eggs, separated
⅔ cup sugar
¼ teaspoon salt
⅓ cup almond meal or ground
    almonds

Position a rack in the center of the oven and preheat the oven to 350°F. Grease an 8" round springform pan and line the pan bottom with a parchment paper round. Set aside.

In the top of a double boiler or a bowl set over simmering water, completely melt the chocolate with the butter, stirring until smooth. Remove from the heat and stir in the espresso and Grand Marnier or orange-flavored liqueur. Set aside.

In a mixing bowl, beat the egg yolks with the sugar and salt until the eggs are thick and pale yellow. Gradually stir in the chocolate mixture, then stir in the almond meal or ground almonds.

In a clean dry bowl, using clean dry beaters, beat the egg whites on medium-high speed until they hold stiff peaks. Stir about one-third of the egg whites into the batter to lighten it. Carefully fold in the remaining egg whites, in two batches, just until well blended.

Pour the batter into the prepared pan and smooth the top with a rubber spatula.

Bake for 30 to 35 minutes, or until the top appears dry but a wooden skewer inserted near the center comes out with crumbs adhered to it. Set the pan on a wire rack to cool for 10 minutes, then release and remove the sides and cool the cake completely. Invert the cake, remove the pan bottom, and carefully peel away the parchment. Reinvert the cake onto a serving plate.

Serving suggestion: Serve with a dollop of Spiked Whipped Cream (see page 27) or Whipped Cream (see page 26) flavored with orange flower water.

Bermudian Rum Cake

Makes one Bundt cake, about 14 servings

This recipe is based on an old favorite of some friends who come from Bermuda. The traditional recipes you will find elsewhere are made with cake mix, but this version is homemade from scratch. The suggested amount of rum in the glaze is generous, so if you'd rather keep the rum flavor mellow, reduce it by half.

FOR THE CAKE
1 cup finely chopped pecans
2 cups unbleached all-purpose flour
1½ cups granulated sugar
1 tablespoon baking powder
½ teaspoon salt
½ cup milk
½ cup orange juice
½ cup vegetable oil
4 eggs, lightly beaten

1 tablespoon freshly grated orange
  zest
⅓ cup dark rum

FOR THE GLAZE
¼ cup (½ stick) unsalted butter,
  softened
½ cup packed brown sugar
2 tablespoons water
¼ cup dark rum

PREPARE THE CAKE

Position a rack in the center of the oven and preheat the oven to 350°F. Grease a 12-cup Bundt pan and sprinkle evenly with the pecans. Set aside.

In a large bowl, whisk together the flour, sugar, baking powder, and salt to combine.

In a separate bowl, whisk together the milk, orange juice, oil, eggs, orange zest, and rum.

Make a well in the center of the dry ingredients and add the liquid mixture. Mix to combine. Slowly pour the batter into the prepared pan, taking care not to dislodge the pecan coating.

Bake for 1 hour, or until a wooden skewer inserted midway between the outer and inner edges of the pan comes out clean. Set the pan on a wire rack and allow the cake to cool completely.

PREPARE THE GLAZE

In a small saucepan, melt the butter over medium heat. Stir in the sugar and water. Bring the mixture to a boil, then lower the heat and simmer, stirring constantly, for 5 minutes. Remove from the heat and stir in the rum.

FINISH THE CAKE

Turn the cake out onto a serving plate. Using a thin wooden skewer, pierce the top of the cake all over. Evenly pour the glaze, a little at a time, over the top of the cake, allowing the glaze to be completely absorbed before adding more.

Serving suggestion: Serve with Spiked Whipped Cream (see page 27) made with rum or an orange-flavored liqueur such as Cointreau.

Earl Grey Tea Cake

Makes one 9" x 5" loaf

There is no reason why a man shouldn't like a slice of this cake, but it's hard to taste this one without thinking about a ladies' luncheon. The essence of bergamot (a type of orange oil used to flavor the tea) is strong and soothing, just like a sweet and milky cup of Earl Grey tea.

FOR THE CAKE
2 cups unbleached all-purpose flour
1 teaspoon salt
1 cup (2 sticks) unsalted butter, softened
1⅓ cups granulated sugar
2 tablespoons loose Earl Grey tea leaves (about 5 tea bags' worth)

1 teaspoon pure vanilla extract
5 eggs

FOR THE GLAZE
¾ cup water
4 Earl Grey tea bags
2 cups confectioners' sugar, sifted

PREPARE THE CAKE

Position a rack in the center of the oven and preheat the oven to 325°F. Grease a 9" x 5" loaf pan and line the pan bottom with parchment paper. Set aside.

In a bowl, whisk together the flour and salt to blend. Set aside.

In the bowl of an electric mixer, beat the butter, sugar, tea leaves, and vanilla on medium speed, until the mixture becomes light and fluffy and the scent of the tea leaves begins to emerge. Add the eggs, one at a time, beating well after each addition.

With the mixer running on low speed, gradually add the flour mixture in three parts, beating until combined, scraping down the sides of the bowl as necessary. Pour the batter into the prepared pan and smooth the top with a rubber spatula.

Bake the cake for 1 hour, or until a wooden skewer inserted in the center comes out clean. Set the cake on a wire rack to cool completely.

PREPARE THE GLAZE

In a small saucepan, bring the water to a boil. Remove the pan from the heat and add the tea bags. Allow the tea to brew for 5 to 7 minutes, or until it is very dark. Remove the tea bags and stir in the sugar.

Turn the cooled cake out of the pan, carefully peel away the parchment, and drizzle the glaze over the cake.

Spiced Bread Pudding

Makes 12–14 servings

Here is a wonderful way to use stale bread. Most types of bread will work very well, as long as they do not contain strongly flavored herbs that could clash with the spices in this recipe. There is no need to remove the crust of even chewy bread since the milk and eggs will soften it. The pudding should be served with one of the recommended sauces or with Whipped Cream (see page 26).

FOR THE CAKE
2 cups granulated sugar
1 cup raisins, currants, dried
 cranberries, or cherries
1 cup chopped toasted pecans
1 teaspoon ground cinnamon
1 teaspoon ground nutmeg
1 teaspoon ground allspice
½ teaspoon ground cardamom
8 cups bite-size pieces stale bread
4 cups whole milk
½ cup (1 stick) butter, melted
3 eggs, beaten
2 tablespoons pure vanilla extract

FOR THE STRAWBERRY SAUCE
4 cups fresh or frozen strawberries
2 teaspoons Grand Marnier or other
 orange-flavored liqueur
½ cup granulated sugar
1 tablespoon cornstarch
2 teaspoons cold water

FOR THE HARD SAUCE
1 cup (2 sticks) unsalted butter,
 softened to room temperature
1 cup confectioners' sugar, sifted
¼ cup dark rum or brandy
1 teaspoon pure vanilla extract
¼ teaspoon freshly grated nutmeg

PREPARE THE CAKE

Do not preheat the oven. Grease a 9" x 13" baking dish and set it aside.

In a large bowl, combine the sugar, raisins (or other dried fruit), pecans, cinnamon, nutmeg, allspice, and cardamom. Add the bread pieces and toss well to combine. Set aside.

In a separate bowl, whisk together the milk, butter, eggs, and vanilla to blend.

Pour the liquid over the bread mixture and stir until the bread pieces have absorbed the liquid. Pour the mixture into the prepared baking dish.

Place on a rack in the center of a cold oven and set the oven to 350°F. Bake for 1½ hours, or until golden brown. Transfer the pan to a wire rack to cool. Serve warm drizzled with either strawberry sauce or hard sauce.

PREPARE THE STRAWBERRY SAUCE

In a medium saucepan, combine the strawberries, Grand Marnier or orange-flavored liqueur, and sugar. Cover and cook over medium heat for 8 to 10 minutes.

In a small bowl, combine the cornstarch with the water and stir to blend. Gradually stir the cornstarch mixture into the strawberry mixture. Cook, stirring, for 2 minutes, then remove from the heat and cool slightly. Serve warm.

PREPARE THE HARD SAUCE

In the bowl of an electric mixer set on medium speed, cream the butter and sugar until light. Add the rum or brandy, vanilla, and nutmeg. Beat for 5 minutes. Serve at room temperature.

Sticky Toffee Cakelets

Makes 8 single-serving cakes

You can turn up the decadence of these gooey cakes by topping them with a scoop of vanilla ice cream before pouring on the sauce–or you can keep things simple by omitting the sauce and serving with a small dollop of Whipped Cream (see page 26).

FOR THE CAKES

1½ cups unbleached all-purpose flour
2 teaspoons baking powder
1½ teaspoons baking soda
½ teaspoon salt
½ cup chopped dried apricots
½ cup pitted, finely chopped dates
¼ cup (½ stick) unsalted butter
¾ cup packed brown sugar
2 eggs
1 teaspoon pure vanilla extract

FOR THE SAUCE

⅔ cup packed brown sugar
6 tablespoons (¾ stick) unsalted butter, softened to room temperature
⅔ cup evaporated milk or heavy cream
1 teaspoon pure vanilla extract

PREPARE THE CAKES

Position a rack in the center of the oven and preheat the oven to 350°F. Grease eight 6-ounce ramekins and line the bottoms with parchment paper rounds.

In a bowl, whisk together the flour, baking powder, baking soda, and salt to blend. Set aside.

In a small bowl, combine the apricots and dates. Pour enough boiling water over the fruit to cover. Set aside.

In the bowl of an electric mixer set on medium speed, or by hand, cream the butter with the sugar for 3 minutes, or until light and fluffy. Add the eggs and vanilla and mix well. Reduce the mixer speed to low and slowly add the dry ingredients. Drain the fruit and gently fold it into the mixture.

Divide the batter among the prepared ramekins, and bake for 15 to 20 minutes, or until the cakes are puffed up and a wooden skewer inserted in the center comes out with moist crumbs attached. (The cakes will fall like a soufflé when removed from the oven.) Set the ramekins on a wire rack to cool slightly. Grasping each ramekin with a dry kitchen towel, run a sharp, thin paring knife around the edge of the ramekin to release. Turn each cakelet out onto a small serving plate, and peel away the parchment.

PREPARE THE SAUCE

Combine the sugar, butter, evaporated milk or cream, and vanilla in a medium saucepan over medium heat and stir until the butter is completely melted and the sugar dissolves. Reduce the heat to a simmer and cook for 5 minutes, or until the sauce darkens to a deep brown color.

To serve, drizzle the warm sauce over the cakes, allowing some sauce to pool in the center where the cakes have fallen.

Tarts

A tart is an elegant piece of handiwork. Once the process of pastry making is mastered, tarts become little works of art that are easy to make and dramatic to give. Greyston does an exceptional job with classic tarts, such as Pecan, Lemon, and Key Lime, the recipes for which are included here. The remaining recipes are inspired by the classics, with flavors and textures not quite as traditional but just as delicious. Unlike cake baking, tart making allows for improvisation—a little less sugar here, an added spice there—and it is with this spirit that the recipes in this chapter were developed. Take care in learning the Tart Pastry recipe on page 18, and then be prepared for lots of praise from the people who are fortunate enough to taste your work.

Pecan Tart

Makes one 9" tart, 8–10 servings

Pecan Tart has always been one of the most popular desserts at the Greyston Bakery, especially around Thanksgiving and Christmas. It keeps well, so on the off chance that you don't finish it, you don't have to worry about it getting soggy. (Photo page 145)

¼ cup (½ stick) unsalted butter
½ cup light corn syrup
⅓ cup packed brown sugar
1½ teaspoons pure vanilla extract
1 teaspoon fresh lemon juice
1 egg

1 egg yolk
¼ teaspoon salt
1 cup pecan pieces, toasted
1 partially baked 9" Tart Pastry (see page 18), cooled
¾ cup pecan halves

Place a rack in the center of the oven and preheat the oven to 350°F.

In a small saucepan, melt the butter over medium heat. Stir in the corn syrup and sugar and bring to a boil. Cook for 1 minute, stirring constantly. Remove the mixture from the heat and allow it to cool for a few minutes. Stir in the vanilla and lemon juice. Set aside.

In a medium bowl, whisk the egg, egg yolk, and salt. Add the butter mixture, a little at a time, stirring until completely combined.

Spread the pecan pieces over the bottom of the tart shell, then arrange the pecan halves on top of the pieces. Slowly and evenly pour the filling over the pecans, tapping down the pecans to coat them.

Bake for 20 to 25 minutes, or until the crust is golden brown and the filling is puffed up. If the pastry edges brown too quickly, cover them with strips of foil or a piecrust shield (see page 9). Remove the pan from the oven and set it on a wire rack to cool.

Serving suggestion: Serve slices topped with vanilla ice cream or Spiked Whipped Cream (see page 27) made with brandy.

Pignoli Tart

Makes one 9" tart, 8–10 servings

This tart is light, with a subtle nutty flavor, and it makes a beautiful presentation. Make sure to toast the pine nuts in a dry pan over medium heat before making the tart; they will not brown much during the baking process.

¾ cup confectioners' sugar, sifted
½ cup almond paste
¼ cup (½ stick) unsalted butter, softened to room temperature
1 tablespoon freshly squeezed lemon juice
1 teaspoon grated lemon zest

2 egg whites
¼ teaspoon salt
2 cups pine nuts (pignoli), lightly toasted
1 partially baked 9" Tart Pastry (see page 18), cooled

Position a rack in the center of the oven and preheat the oven to 350°F.

In the bowl of an electric mixer set on medium speed, cream together the sugar, almond paste, and butter. Add the lemon juice and lemon zest and continue to beat until well combined.

In a clean dry bowl, with clean dry beaters, beat the egg whites and salt on medium-high speed until they hold stiff peaks.

Stir about one-third of the egg whites into the butter mixture to lighten. Fold the remaining whites into the butter mixture, in two batches, until blended completely. Stir in the pine nuts, then pour the filling into the tart shell.

Bake for 30 minutes, or until the filling is lightly browned and set. Remove the pan from the oven and set it on a wire rack to cool completely.

Serving suggestion: *Top with Spiked Whipped Cream (see page 27) or Crème Fraîche (see page 28) with lemon zest.*

Toasted Caramel Almond Tart

Makes one 9" tart, 8–10 servings

For almond lovers only, this tart is pure almond flavor bound together with a deep, sticky caramel filling.

FOR THE PASTRY
½ cup almond flour or finely ground
    blanched almonds
½ cup unbleached all-purpose flour
3 tablespoons confectioners' sugar
½ teaspoon salt
6 tablespoons (¾ stick) unsalted
    butter, chilled
2 egg yolks, lightly beaten

FOR THE FILLING
3 tablespoons + ¼ cup water
½ cup granulated sugar
¼ cup (½ stick) unsalted butter
¼ cup heavy cream
1 teaspoon almond extract
¼ teaspoon salt
2 cups sliced almonds, toasted

PREPARE THE PASTRY

Position a rack in the center of the oven and preheat the oven to 350°F.

In a large bowl, whisk together the almond flour or almonds, all-purpose flour, sugar, and salt to blend. Add the butter and egg yolks, working the dough with your fingertips until crumbly.

Press the dough into a 9" tart pan with a removable bottom. Pierce the bottom of the pastry several times with a fork, then refrigerate it for at least 30 minutes.

Line the chilled dough with foil or parchment paper and fill with pie weights, dry beans, or uncooked rice. Bake for 10 minutes, carefully remove the pie weights, and bake 5 minutes longer. Place the pan on a wire rack to cool.

PREPARE THE FILLING

In a small saucepan, combine the 3 tablespoons of water and the sugar. Cook over medium heat, stirring constantly, until the sugar is completely dissolved.

Raise the heat slightly and bring the mixture to a boil. Cook and stir until the liquid is light golden in color. Remove the pan from the heat and stir in the butter until it is melted. Stir in the ¼ cup water, the cream, almond extract, and salt until the mixture is well blended. Stir in the almonds. If there are lumps in the caramel, return the pan to high heat for a few seconds to melt them.

Pour the filling into the pastry shell and bake for 30 minutes. Set the pan on a wire rack to cool. Serve warm or at room temperature.

Serving suggestion: *Serve with a generous dollop of Whipped Cream (see page 26) or Spiked Whipped Cream (see page 27) made with amaretto, or a scoop of ice cream lightly drizzled with Caramel Sauce (see page 25).*

Spiced Sugar Tartlets

Makes six 4" single-serving tartlets

This is a wonderful dessert any time of the year, but surely these are the sugar-plums spoken of in "The Night Before Christmas."

If you have the Tart Pastry on hand, these are simple to prepare in a pinch.

FOR THE PASTRY
1 recipe Tart Pastry (see page 18),
    wrapped in plastic and chilled at
    least 1 hour

FOR THE TOPPING
½ cup sugar
¼ teaspoon ground cinnamon
¼ teaspoon ground cardamom
⅛ teaspoon freshly ground nutmeg
2 tablespoons butter, chilled

FOR THE FILLING
3 eggs, lightly beaten
⅓ cup sugar
¼ cup very finely chopped almonds
6 tablespoons (¾ stick) unsalted
    butter, melted and cooled
¼ teaspoon salt
1 tablespoon finely grated lemon zest

PREPARE THE PASTRY

Place a rack in the center of the oven and preheat the oven to 425°F.

Divide the pastry dough into 6 equal portions and roll out to form ¼"-thick disks. Press the dough into six 4" metal tart forms. Bake for 10 minutes. Remove them from the oven and set them on a wire rack to cool completely.

PREPARE THE TOPPING

In a small bowl, use your fingertips to work the sugar, cinnamon, cardamom, and nutmeg into the chilled butter. Set aside.

PREPARE THE FILLING

In a medium bowl, mix the eggs, sugar, almonds (these can be run through a food processor for 10 to 15 seconds), butter, salt, and lemon zest. Pour the filling into the cooled tart shells. Return the tarts to the oven and bake for 20 minutes, or until the filling is set around the edges but the centers jiggle when gently shaken.

Sprinkle the topping over the tartlets and return them to the oven to bake for 10 minutes, or until the filling is completely set and the topping is melted and lightly browned.

Serving suggestion: Serve with Whipped Cream (see page 26) and a light drizzle of Caramel Sauce (see page 25).

Tarte Tatin

Makes one 10" tart, about 10 servings

A long cooking time turns the butter, sugar, and apple juices in this recipe into a delicious caramel that floods the apples when the tart is inverted. The French call it *Tarte des Demoiselles Tatin*, after two unmarried sisters who lived in the Loire Valley and earned a living selling these treats. (Photo page 146)

1 recipe Tart Pastry (see page 18), wrapped in plastic and chilled at least 1 hour
1¼ cups sugar
½ cup water
5 tablespoons unsalted butter, cut into small pieces

6 to 8 medium apples (such as Gala, Fuji, or Granny Smith), peeled, cored, and cut lengthwise into quarters

Roll out the pastry dough into an 11" circle. Place on a piece of parchment paper and chill in the refrigerator.

Place a rack in the center of the oven and preheat the oven to 425°F.

In a 10" x 2" ovenproof skillet or a 3-quart round flameproof casserole, combine the sugar and water and stir over medium-low heat for 10 to 15 minutes, until deep golden in color. Stir in the butter until melted.

Arrange as many apple quarters, cut sides down, as will fit on the bottom of the pan, packing them snugly in concentric circles. Fill in any gaps with pieces of apple cut to fit.

Cook over moderately high heat, undisturbed, for 18 to 25 minutes, until the juices are deep golden and bubbling.

Remove the dough from the refrigerator, and lay it over the pan so that there is overlap all around. Trim the overlap by running a rolling pin across the top so that it slices off any extra dough. Reserve the dough scraps for another use (see

"What to Do with Leftover Tart Pastry," page 19). Carefully remove the dough from the pan and return it to the parchment. Refrigerate.

Bake the apples in the skillet for 45 minutes. Remove the pan from the oven and set it on a wire rack to cool slightly. Carefully place the pastry dough on top, fitting it into the shape of the pan. Return the pan to the oven and bake for 20 minutes, or until the pastry is golden. Cool the pan on a wire rack for at least 30 minutes.

Carefully run a small thin knife around the edge of the skillet to loosen the pastry. Place a large platter over the pan and carefully invert the pan and platter together. Remove the pan. Replace any apples that may have fallen out. Serve warm.

Serving suggestion: *Serve each slice topped with a scoop of vanilla ice cream, a dollop of Crème Fraîche (see page 28), or a drizzle of Caramel Sauce (see page 25)—or a little bit of all three!*

Free-Form Apple Tart

Makes one 6" x 12" tart, 6–8 servings

A free-form tart is a nice departure from a traditional tart. Because there is little in the filling aside from the apples, it does not get too soggy, so it holds together nicely. It's beautiful served in thin slices topped with lightly whipped cream.

1 recipe Tart Pastry (see page 18), wrapped in plastic and chilled at least 1 hour

2–3 large apples (about 1 pound), such as Rome Beauty, Jonagold, Granny Smith, pippin, Gala, Cortland, or Winesap

2–4 tablespoons brown sugar, depending on sweetness of apples

½ teaspoon pure almond extract

⅓ cup sliced almonds, toasted

3 tablespoons unsalted butter, chilled and cut into small pieces

¼ cup Apricot Glaze (see page 22)

Position a rack in the center of the oven and preheat the oven to 400°F. Line a baking sheet with parchment paper. Set aside.

On a large wooden cutting board (preferable to a stationary work space), roll out the pastry dough to a rough 9" x 15" rectangle. (If the dough splits or becomes too soft to work with, transfer the board with the dough to the refrigerator and chill for 5 to 10 minutes.) Transfer the dough to the prepared baking sheet. Form a shallow lip by folding over the edges on each side of the dough rectangle. (For a less rustic look, trim the sides and create an even lip with the dough scraps. If desired, create a decorative edge by pressing all around with the tines of a fork or by crimping the dough between your index finger and thumb to create a fluted edge.) The final crust should measure roughly 6" x 12".

Pierce the bottom of the dough with a fork and refrigerate for 10 minutes.

Peel, core, and quarter the apples, then slice them into ⅛" or smaller wedges (a mandoline works well here). In a medium bowl, gently toss the apple slices with the sugar and almond extract. Neatly arrange the slices, overlapping as you go, in two lengthwise rows in the tart shell. Sprinkle or tuck the almonds among the apples and dot the top of the tart with the butter.

Bake for 45 to 50 minutes, or until the crust is golden brown and the apples have some color. Remove the baking sheet from the oven and set on a wire rack to cool to a warm temperature.

In a small pan, warm the Apricot Glaze, then brush it over the top of the tart. Serve warm.

Serving suggestion: *Serve thin slices topped with Spiked Whipped Cream (see page 27) made with Calvados or brandy or with a drizzle of Caramel Sauce (see page 25).*

Peach Crème Brûlée Tart

Makes one 9" tart, 8–10 servings

With a simple custard filling, accented with puréed peaches, this tart makes a great summer dessert.

....

2 small peaches + 1 for garnish (optional)
¼ cup + 3 tablespoons sugar
2 tablespoons unbleached all-purpose flour
⅛ teaspoon salt

2 eggs, separated
⅓ cup whole milk
½ teaspoon pure vanilla extract
1 partially baked 9" Tart Pastry (see page 18), cooled

....

Position a rack in the center of the oven and preheat the oven to 425°F.

Bring a medium saucepan of water to a boil. Using a slotted spoon, lower the 2 peaches into the water for 1 minute, then carefully remove with the slotted spoon. Allow the peaches to cool, then slip off the skins. Halve and pit the peaches and cut into chunks.

In a blender or food processor, add the peach chunks. Process until puréed and set aside. (You should have about ½ cup of peach purée.)

In a medium bowl, whisk together ¼ cup sugar, the flour, and salt to blend well. Set aside.

In another medium bowl, beat the egg yolks, then mix in the milk, vanilla, and peach purée until well combined. Slowly whisk this mixture into the dry ingredients until blended.

In a clean dry bowl, whisk the egg whites until soft peaks form. Gently but thoroughly stir the egg whites into the peach mixture. Pour it into the tart shell.

Bake the tart for 10 minutes, then reduce the temperature to 350°F. Continue baking for 20 to 25 minutes, or until the tart is nearly set but still jiggles slightly when gently shaken. Remove the pan from the oven and set on a wire rack to cool to room temperature. Chill the tart for at least 2 hours.

Preheat the broiler. Evenly sprinkle the remaining 3 tablespoons sugar over the tart. Cover the crust edges with strips of foil or piecrust shields (see page 9). Set the tart under the broiler for 20 seconds, or just until the sugar caramelizes, watching carefully to prevent burning.

Allow the tart to cool to room temperature before serving. Pit and slice the remaining peach and use slices as a garnish, if desired.

Serving suggestion: Serve with a dollop of Whipped Cream (see page 26) or Crème Fraîche (seee page 28).

Apricot Galette

Makes one 8" tart, 6–8 servings

During the summer when apricots are in season, this rustic tart is a must. Be sure to select the most ripe, flavorful apricots.

1 recipe Tart Pastry (see page 18), wrapped in plastic and chilled at least 1 hour
⅓ cup packed brown sugar
3 tablespoons very finely chopped toasted pistachios (optional)
2 tablespoons unbleached all-purpose flour

⅛ teaspoon freshly ground nutmeg
⅛ teaspoon salt
1½ pounds ripe apricots, pitted and cut into eighths
1 tablespoon heavy cream
1 tablespoon granulated sugar

Place a rack in the center of the oven and preheat the oven to 400°F. Line a baking sheet with parchment paper. Set aside.

On a large wooden cutting board, roll out the pastry dough to a 12" circle. (If the dough splits or becomes too soft to work with, transfer the board with the dough to the refrigerator and chill for 5 to 10 minutes.) Transfer the dough to the prepared baking sheet.

In a large bowl, combine the brown sugar, pistachios if using, flour, nutmeg, and salt. Toss to combine. Add the apricots and toss until evenly coated.

Mound the fruit mixture in the center of the crust, leaving a 2" border of dough. Fold the edges over the filling, pinching pleats in the crust as you proceed. Brush the dough with the cream, then sprinkle with the granulated sugar.

Bake for 40 minutes, or until the crust is golden brown. Remove the pan from the oven and set it on a wire rack for a few minutes to cool slightly. Slip the parchment with the tart off the baking sheet onto the wire rack and allow the tart to cool completely, or serve warm.

Serving suggestion: Serve with Whipped Cream (see page 26) or Spiked Whipped Cream (see page 27) made with brandy, Crème Fraîche (see page 28), or a scoop of vanilla ice cream.

Poached Pear Tart

Makes one 9" tart, 8–10 servings

This is a great tart to make during the late fall and early winter when pears are at their best and spices such as cinnamon and star anise are well matched by the cooling weather.

2 cups fruity red wine, such as
    Zinfandel or Beaujolais
1 cup granulated sugar
2 cinnamon sticks, broken in half
4 whole star anise
Zest of 1 orange
5 firm small pears, peeled, quartered,
    and cored

½ cup heavy cream
¼ cup confectioners' sugar
1 teaspoon pure almond extract
    or 2 tablespoons almond liqueur,
    such as Amaretto
½ cup Apricot Glaze (see page 22)
1 fully baked 9" Tart Pastry
    (see page 18), cooled

In a large heavy saucepan, combine the wine, granulated sugar, cinnamon sticks, star anise, and orange zest. Cover and bring to a simmer over medium heat. Add the pears, pouring in a little water or more wine, if necessary, to completely cover the pears. Return the mixture to a simmer, then cover and simmer for 15 to 20 minutes, or until the pears are tender. Remove the pan from the heat and allow the pears to cool in the liquid for at least 2 hours, or up to 2 days in the refrigerator.

Using a slotted spoon, transfer the pears to a plate and pat them dry. Slice them thinly and set aside.

In the bowl of an electric mixer, combine the cream and confectioners' sugar and beat until stiff peaks form. Stir in the almond extract or liqueur.

Brush a thin coat of the glaze on the bottom of the cooled tart shell. Spread the cream mixture over the bottom of the tart shell in an even layer. Arrange the pear slices on top, small ends facing the center. Arrange as many slices as necessary across the center to cover any bare spots.

Carefully brush the pear slices with the remaining glaze. Chill for at least 30 minutes before serving.

Italian Plum Tart

Makes one 9" tart, 8–10 servings

In most of the United States, Italian prune plums are in season in August and September. If you cannot find them, you can make the tart with regular black plums, but try to select the smallest fruit possible. The flavor of the prune plums is far superior, so do what you can to find the real thing.

¾ cup sugar
3 tablespoons unbleached all-purpose flour
2 teaspoons ground cinnamon
1 recipe Tart Pastry (see page 18), formed into a shell, covered in plastic, and chilled at least 1 hour

20–24 small Italian prune plums or 12–15 small black plums
2 tablespoons unsalted butter, chilled and cut into small pieces

Place a rack in the center of the oven and preheat the oven to 425°F.

In a small bowl, whisk together the sugar, flour, and cinnamon to blend. Remove the plastic from the pastry and pierce the bottom with a fork in several places. Evenly sprinkle one-quarter of the sugar mixture over the pastry bottom.

Slice the plums in half lengthwise and discard the pits. Arrange the plum halves in concentric circles over the mixture. Sprinkle the remaining sugar mixture evenly over the plums. Dot the top with the butter.

Bake for 10 minutes, then lower the oven temperature to 350°F and bake for another 30 to 35 minutes. If the crust begins to brown too quickly, cover it with a piecrust shield or strips of foil.

Serving suggestion: *Serve with vanilla ice cream or Crème Fraîche (see page 28).*

Sugared Four-Berry Tart

Makes one 9" tart, 8-10 servings

Show off the best of spring and summer with this brilliant jewel-toned tart. (Photo page 73)

1¼ cups whole milk
⅓ cup heavy cream
5 egg yolks
½ cup granulated sugar
¼ cup cornstarch
2 tablespoons unsalted butter,
    softened

1 tablespoon pure vanilla extract
1 fully baked 9" Tart Pastry
    (see page 18), cooled
3 cups mixed fresh berries, such as
    blueberries, raspberries,
    blackberries, and sliced strawberries
3 tablespoons confectioners' sugar

In a medium saucepan, bring the milk and cream to a boil over medium-high heat. Remove from the heat and set aside.

In a medium bowl, with a fork, blend the egg yolks, granulated sugar, and cornstarch until pale yellow. Gradually whisk in the hot milk mixture. Return the mixture to the saucepan and cook, stirring constantly, over medium-low heat, for 5 minutes, or until the mixture thickens and comes to a boil. (Make sure no custard builds up in the corners of the pan.) Remove the custard from the heat and whisk in the butter and vanilla.

Pour the mixture through a sieve into a bowl and place a piece of plastic wrap directly on top of the custard to prevent a skin from forming. Allow the custard to cool for 1 hour, then chill it in the refrigerator at least 1 hour longer.

Spread the chilled custard over the bottom of the tart shell. Mound with the berries as high as possible, without pushing them down into the custard, about 2" high in the center and 1" around the edges. Dust with the confectioners' sugar before serving.

Serving suggestions: *Decorate the tart with mint or berry leaves.*

French Fruit Tart

This classic French fruit dessert is best in summer. The fruits listed in the recipe are merely suggestions. If you use stone fruits such as apricots or peaches, poach them briefly in simmering water if they are not ripe.

1¼ cups milk
⅓ cup heavy cream
5 egg yolks
½ cup sugar
¼ cup cornstarch
2 tablespoons unsalted butter,
   softened to room temperature
1 tablespoon pure vanilla extract
1 fully baked 9" Tart Pastry
   (see page 18), cooled

1 pint strawberries, stemmed and
   halved
1 cup seedless green and/or black
   grapes, halved
2 kiwifruits, peeled and sliced
   ¼" thick
1 large peach, peeled, pitted, and
   sliced ½" thick
¼ cup Apricot Glaze (see page 22)

In a medium saucepan, bring the milk and cream to a boil over medium-high heat. Remove from the heat.

In a medium bowl, using a fork, blend the egg yolks, sugar, and cornstarch until pale yellow. Gradually whisk in the hot milk mixture. Return the mixture to the saucepan and cook over medium-low heat for 5 minutes, or until the cream thickens and boils, stirring constantly and thoroughly, making sure no custard builds up in the corners of the pan. Remove the pan from the heat. Whisk in the butter and vanilla.

Pour the mixture through a sieve into a bowl and place a piece of plastic wrap directly on top of the custard to prevent a skin from forming. Allow the custard to cool for 1 hour, then chill in the refrigerator at least 2 hours. Spread the chilled custard evenly over the bottom of the tart shell. Mound with the fresh fruit.

In a small saucepan, heat the Apricot Glaze. Brush the warm glaze over the fruit before serving.

Rhubarb Strawberry Tart

Makes one 9" tart, 8–10 servings

So pretty in pink . . . and red, this is the perfect tart to make at the beginning of summer, when both rhubarb and strawberries are at their best. (Photo page 76)

⅓ cup sugar
½ cup water
1¼ pounds fresh rhubarb, trimmed
  and cut diagonally into
  ¼"-thick pieces (about 5 to 6 cups)

1 pint strawberries
1 fully baked 9" Tart Pastry
  (see page 18), cooled

In a heavy saucepan, combine the sugar and water. Stir over medium-low heat until the sugar dissolves. Add the rhubarb, increase the heat, and bring to a boil. Reduce the heat to medium-low, cover, and simmer for 5 minutes, or until the rhubarb is just beginning to soften. Remove the pan from the heat. Let stand, covered, for 10 minutes, or until the rhubarb is tender.

Set a mesh strainer over a medium bowl and drain the rhubarb, reserving the liquid. Allow the rhubarb to cool completely. In a small saucepan, simmer the reserved liquid over medium-low heat for 5 minutes, or until it is reduced to a thick syrup. Set the syrup aside and allow it to cool completely.

Meanwhile, wash and hull the strawberries. Thinly slice the strawberries lengthwise. Nibble on the two end pieces of each strawberry.

Spread the cooled rhubarb evenly over the bottom of the tart shell. Arrange the strawberry slices in concentric circles over the rhubarb filling, covering it completely. Brush or spoon the cooled syrup over the top of the strawberries. Chill before serving.

Serving suggestion: Top slices with a dollop of Whipped Cream (see page 26), Crème Fraîche (see page 28), or vanilla or strawberry ice cream.

Strawberry Custard Tart

Makes one 9" tart, 8–10 servings

Make this tart when strawberries are at their best in early summer. Use the sweetest deep-red strawberries you can find; organic berries are best. This tart makes a lovely ending to a summertime meal.

....

1 cup whole milk
⅓ cup heavy cream
5 egg yolks
½ cup sugar
¼ cup cornstarch
2 tablespoons butter, softened to
    room temperature
3 tablespoons kirsch or other
    fruit-based liqueur

1 teaspoon pure vanilla extract
1 pound small fresh strawberries,
    washed
1 fully baked 9" Tart Pastry
    (see page 18), cooled
¼ cup Red Currant Glaze (see page 23)

....

In a medium saucepan, bring the milk and cream to a boil over medium-high heat. Remove from the heat and set aside.

In a medium bowl, with a fork, blend the egg yolks, sugar, and cornstarch until pale yellow. Gradually whisk in the hot milk mixture. Return the mixture to the saucepan and cook, stirring constantly, over medium-low heat for 5 minutes, or until the mixture thickens and comes to a boil. (Make sure the custard does not build up in the corners of the pan.) Remove the custard from the heat and whisk in the butter, kirsch, and vanilla.

Pour the mixture through a sieve into a bowl and place a piece of plastic wrap directly on top of the custard to prevent a skin from forming. Allow the custard to cool for 1 hour, then chill it in the refrigerator at least 1 hour longer.

Thinly slice enough strawberries to line the bottom of the tart shell, and arrange them in one layer. Carefully spread the chilled custard in an even layer over the berries.

Take a thin slice from the stem end of each remaining strawberry so they will sit upright. Arrange them, cut sides down, in concentric circles on top of the custard.

In a small saucepan over low heat, or in a microwaveable bowl in a microwave oven, heat the glaze for a few minutes, or just until it reaches spreading consistency. Pour or brush the glaze evenly over the berries. Return the tart to the refrigerator until it is ready to serve.

Serving suggestion: Garnish with mint or strawberry leaves and serve with fresh Whipped Cream (see page 26) or Crème Fraîche (see page 28).

Key Lime Tart

Makes one 9" tart, 8–10 servings

If possible, use real key limes, which are sometimes found in markets but can also be ordered online through stores such as Melissa's/World Variety Produce (www.melissas.com). It is also possible to buy bottled key lime juice, but make sure to buy a brand that does not have artificial preservatives added. Otherwise, you're better off substituting regular limes.

FOR THE CRUST

1¼ cups graham cracker crumbs (from about ten 2½" x 5" crackers)
¼ cup finely chopped almonds
2 tablespoons sugar
¼ teaspoon salt
6 tablespoons (¾ stick) unsalted butter, melted

FOR THE FILLING

3 eggs, separated
1 (14-ounce) can sweetened condensed milk
⅔ cup fresh lime juice (from about 13 key limes or 6 to 7 regular limes), see note
1 tablespoon grated lime zest
⅛ teaspoon salt

PREPARE THE CRUST

Position a rack in the center of the oven and preheat the oven to 350°F.

In a food processor, combine the graham cracker crumbs, almonds, sugar, and salt. Add the butter and pulse briefly to combine. Transfer the crumbs to a 9" tart pan with a removable bottom and press the crumbs evenly onto the bottom and sides. (If you don't want your hands to get covered in crumbs, place plastic wrap over the crumbs as you press them into the pan.)

Bake the crust for 10 minutes, or until it begins to darken in color and gives off a rich, nutty scent. Remove the pan from the oven and set it on a wire rack to cool.

PREPARE THE FILLING

In the bowl of an electric mixer, beat the egg yolks until they are thick. Add the condensed milk, lime juice, and lime zest and mix until well combined.

In a clean dry bowl with clean dry beaters, beat the egg whites with the salt on medium-high speed until they hold stiff peaks. In three batches, carefully fold the egg whites into the lime mixture until blended.

Transfer the mixture to the crust and bake for 15 to 20 minutes, or until the filling is barely set.

Note: *To get the most juice from the limes, grate the zest from the limes first. Then microwave the limes on high for 30 to 45 seconds to warm them slightly before juicing.*

Serving suggestion: *Garnish the tart with Candied Citrus Slices (see page 30) made with limes and serve slices topped with a dollop of softly Whipped Cream (see page 26).*

Tropical Custard Tart

Makes one 9" tart, 8–10 servings

This tart makes a great ending to a poolside or other outdoor meal. Use the ripest fruit possible; often, fruit purchased a few days before using is your best bet.

1¼ cups whole milk
⅓ cup heavy cream
5 egg yolks
⅔ cup sugar
¼ cup cornstarch
2 tablespoons unsalted butter, softened to room temperature
3 tablespoons dark rum
½ teaspoon coconut extract
½ cup + 3 tablespoons sweetened flaked coconut

1 fully baked 9" Tart Pastry (see page 18), cooled
½ pineapple, halved lengthwise, cored, and cut crosswise into ¼"-thick slices
1 mango, peeled, halved, and cut crosswise into ¼"-thick slices
¼ cup Apricot Glaze (see page 22)

In a medium saucepan, bring the milk and cream to a boil over medium-high heat. Remove from the heat and set aside.

In a medium bowl, using a fork, blend the egg yolks, sugar, and cornstarch until pale yellow. Gradually whisk in the hot milk mixture. Return the mixture to the saucepan and cook, stirring constantly, over medium-low heat, for 5 minutes, or until the mixture thickens and comes to a boil. (Make sure the custard does not build up in the corners of the pan.) Remove the custard from the heat and whisk in the butter, rum, and coconut extract.

Pour the mixture through a sieve into a bowl, stir in the ½ cup coconut, and place a piece of plastic wrap directly on top of the custard to prevent a skin from forming. Allow the custard to cool for 1 hour, then transfer to the refrigerator and chill for 2 hours.

Spread the chilled custard evenly in the tart shell. Arrange the pineapple and mango in circles on top of the filling.

In a small saucepan over low heat or in a microwaveable bowl in the microwave, heat the glaze for a few minutes, or just until it reaches spreading consistency. Pour or brush the glaze evenly over the fruit. Toast the remaining 3 tablespoons coconut and sprinkle over the tart. The Tropical Custard Tart should be served at room temperature or chilled.

Banana Rum Tart

Makes one 9" tart, 8–10 servings

For those who love a banana cream pie but don't want such a mouthful of super-sweet banana filling, this tart is for you. There is just a thin layer of custard that's not too sweet but still full of banana flavor. Think of it as a banana crème brûlée, with a little kick of rum.

FOR THE CRUST
1½ cups graham cracker crumbs
    (about twelve 2½" x 5" crackers)
5 tablespoons unsalted butter,
    melted
¼ cup granulated sugar
¼ teaspoon salt

FOR THE FILLING
1¼ pounds (about 3 large) firm but
    ripe bananas, peeled, halved
    crosswise, and sliced lengthwise
    into ¼"-thick pieces
1 cup heavy cream
¼ cup granulated sugar
2 tablespoons cornstarch
2 tablespoons rum
2 egg yolks
3 tablespoons packed brown sugar

PREPARE THE CRUST

Position a rack in the center of the oven and preheat the oven to 350°F.

In a food processor, combine the graham cracker crumbs, butter, sugar, and salt. Process to blend completely. Press the mixture onto the bottom and up the sides of a 9" tart pan with a removable bottom. Bake for 15 minutes, or until the crust begins to darken. Remove the pan from the oven and set it on a wire rack to cool.

Arrange half of the banana slices over the bottom of the prepared crust.

In a medium bowl, combine the cream, granulated sugar, cornstarch, rum, and egg yolks, beating until smooth. Slowly pour the custard over the bananas and crust.

Bake for 20 minutes, or until the filling is puffy and starting to set. Remove the tart from the oven and carefully arrange the remaining banana slices across the top. Sprinkle the top of the tart with the brown sugar. Return the tart to the oven and bake 10 to 15 minutes longer, until the sugar is melted and it begins to bubble.

Remove the pan from the oven and set it on a wire rack to cool. Serve the tart warm or at room temperature.

Serving suggestion: *Serve with a dollop of Spiked Whipped Cream (see page 27) made with rum or a scoop of vanilla ice cream.*

Drunken Grape Tart

Makes one 9" tart, 8–10 servings

Here is something light and unique to serve any time of year. It also goes well with a cheese course as dessert. The flavor of the wine really comes through, so be sure to use the best-quality wine possible for both the custard and the glaze.

⅔ cup heavy cream
2 tablespoons cornstarch
3 egg yolks
½ teaspoon pure vanilla extract
¾ cup sweet white wine, such as
    Muscat or Sauternes
½ cup + 2 tablespoons sugar
3 tablespoons unsalted butter,
    softened to room temperature

¼ cup red wine or port
1 tablespoon freshly grated orange
    zest
1 fully baked 9" Tart Pastry (see page
    18), cooled
1½ cups seedless grapes (any variety or
    a mixture), halved lengthwise

In a medium bowl, whisk together the cream, cornstarch, egg yolks, and vanilla for 2 minutes, or until well combined. Set aside.

In a medium saucepan, bring the white wine to a boil and simmer for 3 minutes, or until reduced by half. Add the ½ cup sugar and the butter. Stir until the butter melts. Return the mixture to a boil, then remove from the heat.

In a slow, steady stream, gradually drizzle the hot wine mixture into the cream mixture while whisking vigorously. Return the mixture to the pan and cook, whisking constantly, over medium-low heat for 1 minute, or just until the mixture thickens. Do not overcook. (If the custard is lumpy, strain through a sieve.) Transfer the custard to a clean bowl and set it aside to cool.

In a small saucepan over medium heat, simmer the red wine with the 2 tablespoons sugar, stirring until slightly thickened. Stir in the orange zest. Set the glaze aside to cool.

Spread the wine custard evenly in the bottom of the tart shell. Arrange the grapes, cut sides down, across the top of the tart in concentric circles. With a spoon, drizzle small amounts of the cooled red wine glaze over the grapes, allowing it to collect in the spaces between the grapes, covering all of the custard. Cover loosely and chill at least 3 hours before serving.

Lemon Tart

Makes one 9" tart, 8–10 servings

A Greyston Bakery favorite since the early days, this tart is nice to serve after a summer luncheon or a heavy winter meal. When they're available, try making it with Meyer lemons.

....

8 egg yolks, at room temperature
¾ cup sugar
⅔ cup fresh lemon juice (from 2 medium lemons)
⅛ teaspoon salt

6 tablespoons (¾ stick) unsalted butter, chilled and cut into tablespoon-size pieces
2 tablespoons finely grated lemon zest
1 fully baked 9" Tart Pastry (see page 18), cooled

....

In a medium saucepan, whisk the egg yolks and sugar for 1 minute, or until the mixture is smooth. Whisk in the lemon juice and salt. Heat on medium-low for 10 minutes, whisking constantly until the custard is thick. Remove the pan from the heat and whisk in the butter one piece at a time. Stir until smooth.

Pour the mixture through a sieve into a small bowl, stir in the lemon zest, and place a piece of plastic wrap directly on top of the custard to prevent a skin from forming.

Chill in the refrigerator until firm, for up to 1 week. To serve, spread the cooled filling in the tart shell.

Serving suggestion: *Garnish with Whipped Cream (see page 26) and Candied Citrus Slices (see page 30) made with lemon.*

Maple Fig Tart

Makes one 9" tart, 8–10 servings

Toward the end of summer, when figs are in season, I try to eat them as much as possible. The flavor of a fresh, ripe fig is unparalleled, and there is very little you need to do to it. With the exception of the crust, this tart is not cooked; instead, fresh figs top a creamy base flavored with lemon zest and orange flower water, which can be found in ethnic groceries and online (see Directory of Sources, page 185).

12–16 ripe figs
⅔ cup Crème Fraîche (see page 28) or
    sour cream
⅔ cup mascarpone cheese
¼ cup maple syrup
2 teaspoons orange flower water

1 teaspoon lemon zest
1 fully baked 9" Tart Pastry (see page
    18), cooled
¼ cup Red Currant Glaze (see page 23)

Cut the stems off the figs (leave the skins on) and slice the figs lengthwise into ¼"-thick pieces.

In a bowl, whisk together the Crème Fraîche or sour cream, mascarpone, maple syrup, orange flower water, and lemon zest to blend. Spread the mixture in the bottom of the tart shell. Arrange the figs decoratively over the filling and top with the glaze. Chill for at least 30 minutes before serving.

Chocolate Walnut Tart

Makes one 9" tart, 8–10 servings

This is an old Greyston favorite, and it's especially popular around the holidays. It is possible to substitute other nuts such as pecans or a mix of nuts; however, try it once before experimenting, and use the best-quality chocolate possible.

6 tablespoons (¾ stick) unsalted butter, softened to room temperature
6 ounces good-quality bittersweet or semisweet chocolate, chopped
¼ cup heavy cream
1 egg

¼ cup packed brown sugar
3 tablespoons light corn syrup
1 teaspoon pure vanilla extract
2 cups chopped toasted walnuts
1 partially baked 9" Tart Pastry (see page 18), cooled

Position a rack in the center of the oven and preheat the oven to 350°F.

In the top of a double boiler or a bowl set over simmering water, combine the butter, 4 ounces of the chocolate, and the cream. Stir until the mixture is melted and smooth. Remove the chocolate mixture from the heat and cool slightly.

In a medium bowl, whisk together the egg, sugar, corn syrup, and vanilla to blend thoroughly. Stir in the chocolate mixture and then the walnuts.

Pour the filling into the tart shell. Bake for 15 to 20 minutes, or until the filling has set. Remove the pan from the oven and place it on a wire rack to cool for at least 30 minutes.

Meanwhile, in a small double boiler or a bowl set over simmering water, melt the remaining 2 ounces chocolate over low heat. Dip a fork into the chocolate and drizzle it back and forth over the tart. Let the finished tart sit for 15 minutes before serving.

Serving suggestion: *Serve with a dollop of Spiked Whipped Cream (see page 27) made with brandy or bourbon.*

Hazelnut Meringue Tart

Makes one 9" tart, 8–10 servings

You've probably never had a tart like this, with a dark chocolate-coated crust and a sweet, puffy top. It bakes up whimsically fluffy, appearing as if it's wearing a beret.

3 ounces semisweet or bittersweet chocolate
1 partially baked 9" Tart Pastry (see page 18), cooled
2 eggs
⅔ cup granulated sugar

1 teaspoon pure vanilla extract
1 cup (about 4 ounces) toasted chopped hazelnuts
½ cup hazelnut halves, toasted and skins removed
2 tablespoons confectioners' sugar

In the top of a double boiler, or in a small bowl set over hot water, melt the chocolate, stirring until smooth. (Alternatively, melt the chocolate in the microwave oven in a microwaveable bowl on medium power, checking and stirring after 2 minutes, and then checking and stirring every 30 seconds, until completely melted.) With a pastry brush, evenly coat the bottom of the tart shell with all of the melted chocolate. Set aside to cool.

In the bowl of an electric mixer set on medium speed, lightly whisk the eggs. Add the granulated sugar and vanilla and whisk for 1 to 2 minutes, until the mixture is very frothy. Remove the bowl from the mixer and fold in the chopped hazelnuts. Pour the filling into the cooled tart shell.

Bake for 35 minutes, or until the filling is starting to puff and the center is almost set. Remove the pan from the oven, and gently arrange the hazelnut halves over the top and bake 5 minutes longer. Remove the pan from the oven and set it on a wire rack to cool completely. Sift the confectioners' sugar over the top before serving.

Chocolate Raspberry Ganache Tart

Makes one 9" tart, about 12 slim servings

For as good as it looks and tastes, this tart is shockingly easy to prepare. For the fresh raspberry garnish, try to select the best quality berries you can find, without any bruising or soft spots. Because the tart has such an intense chocolate flavor, it is suggested to serve 12, although you can certainly slice it into pieces as large as your chocolate-loving heart desires.

....

1¼ cups heavy cream
2 tablespoons unsalted butter
12 ounces good-quality bittersweet or semisweet chocolate, chopped
2 tablespoons raspberry liqueur, such as framboise, or other fruit liqueur

1 fully baked 9" Tart Pastry (see page 18), cooled
½ cup fresh raspberries
1 tablespoon confectioners' sugar

....

In a small saucepan on medium-low heat, bring the cream and butter to a boil.

Place the chocolate in a bowl and pour the hot cream mixture on top. Mix until smooth. Stir in the liqueur. Allow the mixture to cool to room temperature, then pour it through a sieve and into the tart shell. Let the tart stand at room temperature for 2 hours, or until the filling has set, or place it in the refrigerator for 1 hour.

To serve, top the tart with the raspberries and dust with the sugar.

PECAN TART (SEE RECIPE, PAGE 112)

145

Tarte Tatin (see recipe, pages 118–19)

PINEAPPLE MACADAMIA UPSIDE-DOWN BARS (SEE RECIPE, PAGES 174–75)

147

New York Cheesecake (see recipe, pages 36–37)

149

Olive Oil and Sherry Soufflé Cake (see recipe, page 91)

EARL GREY TEA CAKE (SEE RECIPE, PAGES 104–105)

151

Triple Chocolate Mousse Cake (see recipe, pages 81–83)

Chocolate Cherry Tart

Makes one 9" tart, about 12 slim servings

This is a very rich dessert for chocolate lovers only. It should be served with something to cut the density of the chocolate experience—whipped cream or, at the very least, a shot of espresso. Because it is so rich, servings can be slight, and one tart can serve 12. (Photo page 80)

FOR THE PASTRY
1¼ cups unbleached all-purpose flour
¼ cup unsweetened cocoa powder
3 tablespoons sugar
¼ teaspoon salt
6 tablespoons (¾ stick) unsalted butter, chilled and cut into small pieces
1 egg
1 tablespoon ice water, or more as needed

FOR THE FILLING
½ cup water
⅓ cup + 2 tablespoons sugar
1 cup dried cherries
¼ cup kirsch or other cherry-flavored liqueur
¾ cup heavy cream
⅓ cup milk
6 ounces good-quality bittersweet or semisweet chocolate, chopped
2 eggs, lightly beaten
¼ teaspoon salt

TO PREPARE THE PASTRY BY HAND

In a bowl, whisk together the flour, cocoa powder, sugar, and salt to blend thoroughly. Using a pastry blender or two knives, cut the butter into the dry ingredients until the mixture resembles coarse crumbs. (Work quickly to prevent the butter from becoming too soft.)

In a small bowl, mix the egg with 1 tablespoon water. Make a well in the crumb mixture and pour in the egg mixture. Use a fork to slowly incorporate. If necessary, add more water, but just enough for the dough to begin forming a ball. Gather the dough into a ball, then flatten into a disk. Wrap in plastic wrap and chill for 1 hour.

continued on page 154

TO PREPARE THE PASTRY IN THE FOOD PROCESSOR

In the bowl of a food processor, combine the flour, cocoa powder, sugar, and salt. Add the butter and process, using short pulses, until the mixture begins to clump and resembles coarse crumbs.

With the machine running, add 1 egg through the feed tube. Add just enough water so the dough begins to form itself into a ball. Remove the dough from the processor, gather it into a ball, and then flatten it into a disk. Wrap the dough in plastic wrap and chill for at least 1 hour.

FORM AND BAKE THE PASTRY SHELL

On a lightly floured work surface, roll the dough out to a rough circle about ¼" thick. Transfer carefully to a 9½" fluted tart pan with a removable bottom. Press the dough lightly but snugly into the edges of the pan. (The dough will reach up and over the sides of the pan.) Roll a rolling pin over the top of the pan to trim the dough flush with the rim. Reserve the dough scraps for another use (see "What to Do with Leftover Tart Pastry," page 19). Lightly pierce the bottom of the dough all over with a fork. Chill for 30 minutes.

Position a rack in the center of the oven and preheat the oven to 425°F.

Line the chilled shell with foil and fill with pie weights, dried beans, or raw rice. Bake for 12 minutes, or until the pastry is set and golden. Remove the pan from the oven and set it on a wire rack to cool. Reduce the oven temperature to 325°F.

PREPARE THE FILLING

In a medium saucepan, combine the water and ⅓ cup sugar. Cook, stirring over medium heat until all of the sugar dissolves and the syrup comes to a boil. Add the dried cherries and kirsch and continue to stir over medium heat for 3 minutes longer. Remove the pan from the heat and allow the mixture to cool for 30 minutes. Cover and refrigerate until completely cool.

In a medium saucepan, bring the cream and milk to a simmer over medium-low heat. Remove the pan from the heat and stir in the chocolate until it is melted and smooth. Cool slightly.

In a bowl, whisk the 2 tablespoons sugar with the eggs and salt for 2 to 3 minutes, or until the eggs begin to thicken. Gradually whisk the eggs into the chocolate mixture.

Drain the cooled cherries, reserving the syrup. Arrange the cherries on the bottom of the tart shell. Slowly pour the chocolate filling over the cherries.

Bake for 15 to 20 minutes, or until the filling has set and the surface of the tart is glossy. Remove the pan from the oven and set it on a wire rack to cool completely.

This tart can be made 1 day ahead, stored in the refrigerator, and covered with plastic wrap. Return to room temperature before serving.

Serving suggestion: Serve slices topped with softly Whipped Cream (see page 26) and chocolate shavings or Chocolate Curls (see page 31).

Cookies and Bars

The Greyston Bakery is most famously known for the delicious baked goods found in Ben & Jerry's ice creams, namely brownies and blondies. These two products inspired the recipes in this chapter. Cookies and bars have long been a favorite of the home baker for their relative ease of preparation, their portability (think picnics, lunch boxes, purse pouches, and suit pockets), and, of course, the joy they bring to both those who prepare them and those who simply indulge.

The Good Cookie

Makes about 3½ dozen

When Ben Cohen of Ben and Jerry's found himself laden with leftover Brazil nut crumbs from his company's Rainforest Crunch candy, he asked if the Greyston Bakery could use them. The bakery created these cookies by substituting nut crumbs for some of the flour. The cookies became famous when the White House ordered them for its famous Easter Egg Roll on the South Lawn in 1993.

1¼ cups unbleached all-purpose flour
1 cup (about 4 ounces) ground Brazil
   or macadamia nuts
1 teaspoon baking powder
½ teaspoon salt
½ cup (1 stick) unsalted butter,
   softened to room temperature

1 cup packed brown sugar
½ cup granulated sugar
1½ teaspoons pure vanilla extract
3 eggs
2 cups (12 ounces) semisweet
   chocolate pieces

Position a rack in the center of the oven and preheat the oven to 375°F. Lightly grease several baking sheets or line them with parchment paper.

In a small bowl, whisk together the flour, ground nuts, baking powder, and salt.

In the bowl of an electric mixer set on medium speed, cream the butter, brown sugar, granulated sugar, and vanilla until light and fluffy.

Reduce the mixer speed to low. Add the eggs, one at a time, beating well and scraping the sides of the bowl after each addition. Gradually beat in the flour mixture. Stir in the chocolate. Refrigerate the dough for 10 minutes.

Drop the dough by rounded tablespoonfuls onto the prepared baking sheets. (If you're not baking all of the cookies at once, keep the extra dough chilled.)

Bake for 12 minutes, or until the cookies are golden brown. Cool the cookies on the baking sheets on wire racks for at least 5 minutes before transferring the cookies to the racks to cool completely.

Oatmeal Chocolate Chunk Cookies

Makes about 2 dozen

Oatmeal raisin cookies are fine, but we all know that people really want chocolate. These cookies combine the heartiness of a traditional oatmeal cookie with chunks of chocolate and a good dose of shredded coconut for more texture and flavor. They will convert any self-avowed oatmeal cookie enemy into an oatmeal cookie lover.

1½ cups unbleached all-purpose flour
1 teaspoon baking soda
1 teaspoon salt
1 cup (2 sticks) unsalted butter, softened to room temperature
1½ cups packed brown sugar
1 egg

1½ teaspoons pure vanilla extract
2 cups old-fashioned rolled oats
¾ cup shredded coconut
7 ounces bittersweet or semisweet chocolate, chopped into small chunks

Position a rack in the center of the oven and preheat the oven to 350°F. Line 2 baking sheets with parchment paper.

In a medium bowl, whisk the flour, baking soda, and salt to blend. Set aside.

In the bowl of an electric mixer set on medium speed, cream the butter and sugar together for 3 minutes, or until light and fluffy. Add the egg and vanilla and continue beating until well combined, scraping down the sides as necessary.

With the mixer on low speed, gradually add the flour mixture, mixing until just combined. With a wooden spoon or rubber spatula, fold in the oats, coconut, and chocolate.

Drop the batter in rounded tablespoons, 2" apart, onto the prepared baking sheets. Bake 12 to 15 minutes, or until the cookies are golden brown. Transfer the cookies to wire racks to cool.

Peanut Butter Cookies

Makes about 3 dozen

A classic snack, peanut butter cookies are shockingly simple to make. Have a few with a glass of milk or crumble them over ice cream.

....

1¼ cups unbleached all-purpose flour
¼ teaspoon baking soda
1¼ cups packed brown sugar
1 cup smooth or crunchy peanut
   butter, at room temperature

¼ cup (½ stick) unsalted butter,
   softened to room temperature
1 egg
1 teaspoon pure vanilla extract

....

Position a rack in the center of the oven and preheat the oven to 350°F.

In a small bowl, whisk together the flour and baking soda to blend.

In the bowl of an electric mixer set on medium speed, cream the sugar, peanut butter, and butter. Add the egg and vanilla and continue beating until just blended. Reduce the mixer speed to low and add the dry ingredients, beating until blended.

Drop by rounded tablespoonfuls onto ungreased baking sheets. Press with the heel of your hand to flatten slightly, then make crisscross marks by pressing the tops of the cookies with the tines of a fork.

Bake for 12 minutes, or until golden brown. Cool the cookies on the baking sheets for a few minutes before transferring the cookies to wire racks to cool completely.

Pecan Tassies

Makes 2 dozen

A tassie is a cookie baked in a mini muffin tin, usually filled with cream cheese, and often having a pecan crust. They make terrific gifts for holiday parties. They don't have many ingredients so they're simple to put together and are out of the oven in less than 15 minutes. This recipe was adapted from a 1930s Iowa cookbook.

½ cup cream cheese, softened to room temperature
½ cup (1 stick) unsalted butter, softened to room temperature
1 cup unbleached all-purpose flour

1½ cups toasted pecans, chopped
¾ cup packed brown sugar
1 tablespoon unsalted butter, melted
1 egg, beaten
½ teaspoon pure vanilla extract

Position a rack in the center of the oven and preheat the oven to 325°F.

In the bowl of an electric mixer set on medium speed, or by hand, cream together the cream cheese, ½ cup butter, and the flour. Press a few tablespoonfuls of the mixture onto the bottom and sides of each cup in a mini muffin tin, forming cups for filling. (You'll need to work in two batches unless you have two tins.)

In another bowl, combine the pecans, sugar, 1 tablespoon butter, egg, and vanilla. Dollop the pecan mixture over the cream cheese cups.

Bake for 10 to 12 minutes, or until the tassie crust is light golden brown. Set the pan on a wire rack to cool completely.

The Great Brownie

Makes 2 dozen

This is a chunkier, more chocolatey version of the famous brownies Greyston makes for Ben & Jerry's Chocolate Fudge Brownie Ice Cream.

1 cup unbleached all-purpose flour
¾ cup unsweetened cocoa powder
½ teaspoon salt
¾ cup (1½ sticks) unsalted butter, softened to room temperature
1½ cups sugar

3 eggs
1 tablespoon pure vanilla extract
7 ounces high-quality bittersweet chocolate, roughly chopped
1 ounce high-quality bittersweet chocolate, finely chopped

Place a rack in the center of the oven and preheat the oven to 325°F. Grease a 9" x 13" baking pan and line it with parchment paper, leaving about 1" of paper overhanging the two long sides.

In a bowl, whisk together the flour, cocoa powder, and salt to blend. Set aside.

In the bowl of an electric mixer set to medium speed, beat the butter and sugar. Beat in the eggs, one at a time. Stir in the vanilla. Gradually mix in the dry ingredients until well combined. Stir in half of the roughly chopped chocolate chunks.

Spread the batter evenly in the prepared pan. Evenly distribute the remaining roughly chopped chocolate chunks over the surface of the batter.

Bake for 35 to 40 minutes, or until the sides of the brownies have begun to pull away slightly and the center tests slightly moist when a wooden skewer is inserted. Remove the pan from the oven and place it on a wire rack to cool completely.

Meanwhile, place the finely chopped chocolate in a heatproof bowl over a saucepan containing about 1" of water. Stir over low heat until the chocolate is melted. Drizzle the chocolate over the cooled brownies. Allow the drizzled chocolate to set. Grasping the edges of the parchment, remove the brownies from the pan and cut into bars.

The Great Blondie

Makes 2 dozen

This chewy, buttery treat was created after The Great Brownie (see page 162) became such a popular dessert. Greyston supplied a simplified version of this recipe for Ben & Jerry's Blondies are a Swirls Best Friend ice cream flavor.

2 cups unbleached all-purpose flour
1 teaspoon salt
¾ cup (1½ sticks) unsalted butter,
  softened to room temperature
¾ cup granulated sugar
¾ cup packed brown sugar

3 eggs
2 teaspoons pure vanilla extract
1 cup semisweet chocolate pieces
1 cup butterscotch pieces
1 cup coarsely chopped walnuts

Position a rack in the center of the oven and preheat the oven to 325°F. Grease a 9" x 13" baking pan or heatproof glass dish. Line the pan with parchment paper, leaving about 1" of paper overhanging the two long sides.

In a bowl, whisk together the flour and salt to blend. Set aside.

In the bowl of an electric mixer set on medium speed, cream the butter, granulated sugar, and brown sugar. Beat in the eggs, one at a time, blending thoroughly and stopping to scrape down the sides of the bowl after each addition. Mix in the vanilla.

Stir in the flour mixture until well combined. Stir in ½ cup of the chocolate pieces, ½ cup of the butterscotch pieces, and ½ cup of the walnuts. Spread the batter evenly in the prepared pan with the back of a spoon or a rubber spatula. Sprinkle the remaining chocolate pieces, butterscotch pieces, and walnuts evenly over the top.

Bake for 30 minutes, or until a wooden skewer inserted near the center comes out clean. Set the pan on a wire rack to cool for 15 minutes. Grasp the edges of the parchment and carefully lift the blondies out of the pan. Cut into bars.

Cheesecake Brownie Bars

Makes 2 dozen

Here is a rich dessert bar that can be dressed up with berries or ice cream for a dinner party or dressed down in a gingham cloth for a picnic. This recipe should be prepared ahead of time to give the cheesecake topping time to set in the refrigerator—at least 6 hours, but preferably overnight.

FOR THE BROWNIE BASE

6 ounces good-quality bittersweet
   chocolate, chopped into 1" pieces
½ cup (1 stick) unsalted butter
1 cup + 2 tablespoons sugar
3 eggs
1½ teaspoons pure vanilla extract
½ teaspoon salt
¾ cup unbleached all-purpose flour

FOR THE CHEESECAKE TOPPING

2 (8-ounce) packages cream cheese,
   softened to room temperature
¾ cup sugar
¼ cup milk
2 eggs
2 teaspoons pure vanilla extract
¼ teaspoon salt

PREPARE THE BROWNIE BASE

Position a rack in the center of the oven and preheat the oven to 350°F. Grease a 9" x 13" baking pan or heatproof glass dish. Line the pan with parchment paper, leaving about 1" of paper overhanging the two long sides.

In a metal bowl set over a pan of barely simmering water (don't let the pan touch the water), combine the chocolate and butter. Stir until the chocolate is melted and the mixture is smooth. Set aside to cool slightly.

In the bowl of an electric mixer set on medium speed, beat the sugar and eggs together until thick and pale yellow in color. Beat in the vanilla and salt. Alternately stir in some of the chocolate mixture and the flour, repeating until all of the ingredients are well combined.

Pour the batter into the prepared pan, and bake for 20 to 25 minutes, or until the batter starts to set. Remove the pan from the oven and set it on a wire rack to allow it to cool slightly.

PREPARE THE CHEESECAKE TOPPING

While the brownie base is baking, cream the cream cheese and sugar in the bowl of an electric mixer set on medium-high speed. Reduce the speed to medium and beat in the milk, eggs, vanilla, and salt. Using a rubber spatula or the back of a spoon, spread the cheesecake topping in an even layer over the partially baked brownie base.

Return the brownie pan to the oven and bake for 40 to 50 minutes, or until the top is puffed and pale golden in color and a wooden skewer inserted near the center comes out with crumbs adhering to it. Set the pan on a wire rack to cool completely, then refrigerate, covered, at least 6 hours or overnight. Remove the brownies from the pan by grasping and lifting the edges of the parchment. Cut into bars.

Macaroon Brownie Bars

Makes 16

For people who like a little coconut with their chocolate, here is a perfectly balanced dessert: a thin brownie layer topped with an equal layer of coconut, reminiscent of a gooey macaroon.

FOR THE BROWNIE BASE
⅔ cup unbleached all-purpose flour
⅓ cup unsweetened cocoa powder
¼ teaspoon salt
½ cup (1 stick) unsalted butter, softened to room temperature
⅔ cup sugar
3 eggs
1 teaspoon pure vanilla extract
½ teaspoon pure almond extract

4 ounces good-quality bittersweet chocolate, chopped into chunks

FOR THE COCONUT TOPPING
2 eggs
⅔ cup sugar
¼ teaspoon pure almond extract
⅓ cup unbleached all-purpose flour
2¼ cups (7 ounces) sweetened flaked coconut

PREPARE THE BROWNIE BASE

Place a rack in the center of the oven and preheat the oven to 350°F. Grease a 9" baking pan and line it with parchment paper, leaving about 1" of paper overhanging the two long sides.

In a bowl, whisk together the flour, cocoa powder, and salt until well blended.

In the bowl of an electric mixer, cream the butter and sugar on medium speed. Add the eggs, one at a time, mixing well after each addition. Stir in the vanilla and almond extract. Gradually mix in the dry ingredients until well combined. Stir in the chocolate.

Spread the batter evenly in the prepared pan. Bake for 20 minutes, or until the sides begin to set but the center is still soft. Remove the pan from the oven and set on a wire rack to cool slightly.

PREPARE THE COCONUT TOPPING

In a bowl, whisk together the eggs and sugar. Stir in the almond extract. Gradually stir in the flour, mixing thoroughly. Stir in the coconut.

Using 2 spoons, gently place spoonfuls of the mixture over the partially baked brownie base and spread evenly with the back of a spoon or a rubber spatula.

Return the pan to the oven and bake for 30 minutes, or until the topping is golden brown and a wooden skewer inserted in the middle comes out almost clean. (Some crumbs will still be attached. Do not overbake.) Remove the pan from the oven and set it on a wire rack to cool completely. Remove the brownies by grasping and lifting the edges of the parchment. Cut into bars.

Gingered Lemon Squares

Makes 2 dozen

It's hard to improve on a good old-fashioned lemon square, but the addition of ginger gives these squares an extra kick. These are just as good as the bars you ate as a child, but they have a touch of sophistication. Feel free to increase or decrease both the ground ginger in the crust and the fresh ginger in the topping for more or less zip.

FOR THE CRUST
2 cups unbleached all-purpose flour
½ cup packed brown sugar
¼ cup confectioners' sugar
1 tablespoon ground ginger
½ teaspoon ground cinnamon
¼ teaspoon salt
¾ cup (1½ sticks) cold unsalted butter, cut into small pieces
1 egg
1–2 tablespoons ice water

FOR THE TOPPING
4 eggs
1½ cups granulated sugar
¾ cup fresh lemon juice
⅓ cup unbleached all-purpose flour
2 tablespoons freshly grated ginger
1 tablespoon freshly grated lemon zest
3 tablespoons confectioners' sugar

PREPARE THE CRUST

Position a rack in the center of the oven and preheat the oven to 350°F. Grease a 9" x 13" baking pan and line it with parchment paper, leaving about 1" of paper overhanging the two long sides.

In the bowl of a food processor, combine the flour, brown sugar, confectioners' sugar, ginger, cinnamon, and salt. Process briefly. Sprinkle the butter on top and pulse until the mixture resembles a coarse meal.

In a small bowl, whisk together the egg and water. Slowly pour the egg mixture through the feed tube, pulsing until the mixture begins to hold together. (If the mixture does not hold together when pressed between your fingers, pulse in more ice water, 1 teaspoon at a time.)

Transfer the mixture to the prepared pan and press evenly onto the bottom of the pan. Bake for 20 minutes, or until golden. Remove the pan from the oven and set it on a wire rack to cool slightly. Reduce the oven temperature to 300°F.

PREPARE THE TOPPING

While the crust is baking, whisk together the eggs and granulated sugar in a bowl until well combined and pale in color. Stir in the lemon juice, flour, ginger, and lemon zest. Pour over the warm crust. Return the pan to the oven, and bake for 30 minutes, or until set.

Remove the pan from the oven and set it on a wire rack, allowing it to cool completely. Remove the squares by grasping and lifting the edges of the parchment. Cut into bars.

Dust the bars with the confectioners' sugar before serving. The bars will keep, covered and chilled, for 3 days.

Lime Bars with White Chocolate

Makes 16

These cookie bars capture the beloved taste of a key lime pie in a little handheld bar, ready to go in a youngster's lunch box or even your briefcase. A drizzle of white chocolate gives it extra crunch and sweetness.

FOR THE CRUST

1½ cups ground graham crackers
   (about twelve 2½" x 5" crackers)
3 tablespoons sugar
1 tablespoon freshly grated lime zest
⅛ teaspoon salt
6 tablespoons unsalted butter, melted

FOR THE TOPPING

2 (8-ounce) packages cream cheese
½ cup sugar
2 egg yolks
½ cup freshly squeezed lime juice
1 tablespoon freshly grated lime zest
4 ounces white chocolate, finely
   chopped

PREPARE THE CRUST

Position a rack in the center of the oven and preheat the oven to 350°F. Grease a 9" baking pan and line it with an 8" x 12" piece of parchment, so that the parchment extends over the opposite sides of the pan. Set aside.

Combine the graham crackers, sugar, lime zest, and salt in a bowl. Pour the butter over the mixture and blend with a fork. Press the mixture into the bottom of the prepared dish. Bake for 10 to 12 minutes, or until the color deepens and the crust becomes fragrant. Remove the pan from the oven and set it aside to cool slightly.

PREPARE THE TOPPING

Meanwhile, in the bowl of an electric mixer set on medium speed, cream together the cream cheese and sugar. Add the egg yolks and continue to mix until blended. Add the lime juice and lime zest and mix until blended.

Pour the mixture over the warm crust and return the pan to the oven. Bake for 30 to 35 minutes, or until the center of the topping is set and the top is beginning to color slightly. Remove the pan from the oven and set it on a wire rack to cool completely.

Set up a small double boiler, or place a metal or heatproof bowl across the top of a pan that has a little simmering water in it. (Make sure the bottom of the bowl doesn't touch the water below.) Allow the bowl to heat over the water. Remove the double boiler from the heat and put the chocolate in the bowl. Stir until it melts. (Be careful not to let water or steam get into the chocolate, as it will cause the chocolate to seize up.)

Decorate the top of the pan of cooled bars with white chocolate by dipping a knife into the melted chocolate and drizzling it decoratively across the bars in diagonal lines to create a grid design.

Remove the lime bars from the pan by grasping and lifting the edges of the parchment. Cut into bars.

Orange Shortbread Bars

Makes 16

Like a buttery shortbread with marmalade topping, this bar has a grown-up flavor that is as good with Mom's cup of after-work tea as it is with the kids' after-school snack.

FOR THE SHORTBREAD BASE

¾ cup orange preserves

2 tablespoons Grand Marnier or other orange-flavored liqueur

¾ cup (1½ sticks) unsalted butter, softened to room temperature

½ cup granulated sugar

½ cup ground almonds

1 tablespoon freshly grated orange zest

1 teaspoon pure almond extract

¼ teaspoon salt

2 cups unbleached all-purpose flour

FOR THE TOPPING

3 tablespoons unbleached all-purpose flour

2 tablespoons packed brown sugar

⅛ teaspoon freshly grated nutmeg

⅛ teaspoon salt

2 tablespoons chilled unsalted butter, diced

2 tablespoons sliced almonds

PREPARE THE SHORTBREAD BASE

Position a rack in the center of the oven and preheat the oven to 350°F. Grease a 9" baking pan and line it with an 8" x 12" piece of parchment so that the parchment extends over the opposite sides of the pan. Set aside.

In a small bowl, combine the preserves and liqueur. Set aside.

In the bowl of an electric mixer set on medium speed, cream the butter and sugar together until light and fluffy. Add the ground almonds, orange zest, almond extract, and salt. Sift in the flour, stirring until the mixture forms a soft dough. Press the dough evenly over the bottom of the prepared pan. Evenly spread the preserves mixture over the dough.

In a bowl, whisk together the flour, sugar, nutmeg, and salt until well blended. Using your fingertips, rub the butter into the dry ingredients until crumbly. Mix in the almonds. Press the topping lightly into the preserves-topped dough.

Bake for 1 hour, or until golden brown. (If the topping begins to burn, cover loosely with foil.) Remove the pan from the oven and set it on a wire rack to cool completely. Remove the bars from the pan by grasping and lifting the edges of the parchment. Cut into bars.

Pineapple Macadamia Upside-Down Bars

Makes 1 to 2 dozen, depending on the topping design

Taking their inspiration from the pineapple upside-down cakes of our grand-mothers' kitchens, these bars offer all the sweet pineapple flavor you need in just a few bites. With a little careful planning, you can arrange a floral design using the pineapple chunks. (Photo page 147)

FOR THE TOPPING

¼ cup (½ stick) unsalted butter, melted
⅔ cup packed brown sugar
60 1" pineapple wedges (from ½ pineapple)
12 macadamia nut halves (or more to taste)

FOR THE CRUST

1¾ cups unbleached all-purpose flour
⅓ cup chopped macadamia nuts
½ cup packed brown sugar
1½ teaspoons baking powder
½ teaspoon salt
¾ cup (1½ sticks) unsalted butter, chilled and cut into small pieces
2 eggs

PREPARE THE TOPPING

Place a rack in the center of the oven and preheat the oven to 350°F. Grease a 9" x 13" baking pan and line it with parchment paper, leaving about 1" of paper overhanging the two long sides.

In a small bowl, combine the butter and sugar and spread the mixture evenly in the prepared pan.

Pat the pineapple pieces dry between several thicknesses of paper towels and arrange them evenly on the sugar mixture, either in 24 equal-size pinwheel designs (see photo, page 147) or scattered in rows, leaving space for slicing the pan's contents into 24 bars of equal size. Arrange the nut halves among the pineapple pieces.

In the bowl of a food processor, combine the flour, nuts, sugar, baking powder, and salt and process until combined. Drop in the butter and eggs, and process until the mixture begins to form small clumps. Press the mixture evenly over the pineapple in the pan. Bake for 25 to 30 minutes, or until golden.

Remove the pan from the oven and set it on a wire rack to cool completely. Carefully remove the bars from the pan by pulling up on the edges of the parchment. Cut into bars, and serve them upside down, with the pineapple design facing up.

Oatmeal Maple Bars

Makes 2 dozen

These bars make a great snack. With the oats, maple, and currants, some might even be tempted to have them for breakfast. (Photo page 148)

FOR THE BARS
1½ cups unbleached all-purpose flour, sifted
1 cup oats
1 teaspoon baking powder
¾ teaspoon salt
1 cup (2 sticks) unsalted butter, softened to room temperature
¾ cup granulated sugar
1 cup pure maple syrup
2 large eggs
2 teaspoons pure vanilla extract

1 tablespoon freshly grated orange zest
½ cup currants
½ cup chopped walnuts

FOR THE GLAZE
¼ cup (½ stick) unsalted butter
3 tablespoons pure maple syrup
3 tablespoons whipping cream
½ cup confectioners' sugar, sifted
24 walnut halves

PREPARE THE BARS

Position a rack in the center of the oven and preheat the oven to 350°F. Grease a 9" x 13" baking pan or heatproof glass dish. Line the pan with parchment paper, leaving about 1" of paper overhanging the two long sides.

Combine the flour, oats, baking powder, and salt in a medium bowl.

In a metal bowl with an electric mixer, beat the butter, sugar, and maple syrup on medium-high speed until light and fluffy. Reduce the speed to low and add the eggs, vanilla, and orange zest, beating well. Stir in the dry ingredients. Fold in the currants and walnuts.

Spread the batter in the prepared pan. Bake for 40 to 45 minutes, or until the top is golden and a wooden skewer inserted in the center comes out clean. Set the pan on a wire rack and allow it to cool completely.

PREPARE THE GLAZE

Melt the butter in a small heavy saucepan. Stir in the maple syrup and cream. Remove the glaze from the heat and add the sugar, whisking until smooth. Allow the glaze to cool for 15 minutes, or until slightly thickened.

FINISH THE BARS

Remove the bars from the pan by grasping and lifting the edges of the parchment. Drizzle the glaze over the bars. Let the bars stand for 10 minutes, or until the glaze has set. Cut into bars and place a walnut half in the center of each bar.

Pumpkin Bars

Makes 2 dozen

Pumpkin pie is too holiday-specific a concoction for those of us who love its taste and wish it could be more of a casual affair. These bars are just like a pie, but you can grab one and pop it into your mouth without having to sit down to dinner with the entire family and do hours of dishes. Some holiday traditions are worth reinventing.

FOR THE BASE
1½ cups unbleached all-purpose flour
½ teaspoon salt
½ teaspoon baking soda
¾ cup (1½ sticks) unsalted butter, softened to room temperature
⅓ cup granulated sugar
⅓ cup packed brown sugar
½ cup finely chopped pecans or walnuts

FOR THE FILLING
1 (8-ounce) package cream cheese, softened to room temperature
¾ cup granulated sugar

1 teaspoon ground ginger
½ teaspoon salt
¼ teaspoon ground cloves
2 eggs, lightly beaten
2 cups (one 15-ounce can) canned pumpkin
¼ cup half-and-half, cream, or evaporated milk

FOR THE TOPPING
¼ cup (½ stick) unsalted butter, melted
¾ cup packed brown sugar
1 cup roughly chopped pecans or walnuts

PREPARE THE BASE

Position a rack in the center of the oven and preheat the oven to 375°F. Grease a 9" x 13" baking pan or heatproof glass dish. Line the pan with parchment paper, leaving about 1" of paper overhanging the two long sides.

In a mixing bowl, whisk together the flour, salt, and baking soda to blend. Set aside.

In the bowl of an electric mixer set on medium speed, cream the butter, granulated sugar, and brown sugar. Gradually add the dry ingredients, mixing until well blended. Stir in the pecans or walnuts. Press the mixture over the bottom of the prepared pan.

Bake for 10 minutes. Remove the pan from the oven and set on a wire rack to cool slightly.

PREPARE THE FILLING

In the bowl of an electric mixer set on medium speed, blend the cream cheese, sugar, ginger, salt, and cloves. Reduce the speed to low and gradually beat in the eggs. Stir in the pumpkin and half-and-half, cream, or milk until well blended.

Gently pour the filling (it will be very soupy) over the partially baked crust. Return the pan to the oven and bake for 50 to 60 minutes, or until it is almost set in the center. Remove the pan from the oven and set aside. Preheat the broiler.

PREPARE THE TOPPING

In a small bowl, toss the butter with the sugar and pecans or walnuts to combine. Sprinkle the topping evenly over the baked bars. Broil a few minutes, or until the topping begins to bubble, watching carefully so it doesn't burn.

Set the pan on a wire rack to cool completely. Run a sharp knife around the pan's edges without the extra parchment, to release. Grasp the edges of the parchment and carefully lift the bars out of the pan. Cut into bars.

Seven-Layer Cookie Bars

Makes 2 dozen

What could be easier . . . or more tempting?

1 cup sweetened flaked coconut
1½ cups graham cracker crumbs (from about fourteen 2½" x 5" crackers)
½ cup (1 stick) unsalted butter, melted
¾ cup semisweet chocolate chips

¾ cup butterscotch chips
¾ cup chopped walnuts
1 (14-ounce) can sweetened condensed milk

Place a rack in the center of the oven and preheat the oven to 350°F. Grease a 9" x 13" baking pan or glass dish. Line the pan with parchment paper, leaving about 1" of paper overhanging the two long sides.

Place the coconut flakes on an ungreased baking sheet and bake for 10 minutes, or until the coconut begins to brown. Remove the baking sheet from the oven, stir the coconut gently with a spatula, and return it to the oven for 5 minutes longer. Remove the coconut from the oven and set it aside to cool.

In a medium bowl, mix the graham cracker crumbs with the butter until the crumbs are moistened. Press the crumb mixture evenly onto the bottom of the prepared pan. Top with layers of the coconut, chocolate chips, butterscotch chips, and walnuts. Pour the condensed milk evenly over the top.

Bake for 30 minutes, or until golden brown. Remove the pan from the oven. and set it on a wire rack to cool completely. Grasp the edges of the parchment and carefully lift the bars out of the pan. Cut into bars.

Toasted Pecan Bars

Makes 16–20

Greyston Bakery board member Rozanne Gold loves these bars because they are so easy to make. She suggests cutting them either into small bars as a kind of brownie or into larger squares served slightly warm and topped with vanilla ice cream.

1½ cups chopped toasted pecans
1 cup graham cracker crumbs
  (from about seven 2½" x 5"
  crackers)
⅔ cup miniature chocolate chips

⅛ teaspoon salt
1 (14-ounce) can sweetened
  condensed milk
1 teaspoon pure vanilla extract

Position a rack in the center of the oven and preheat the oven to 350°F. Grease a 9" baking dish and line it with parchment paper, leaving about 1" of paper overhanging the two long sides.

In a large bowl, combine the pecans, graham cracker crumbs, chocolate chips, and salt. Stir in the condensed milk and vanilla and mix until thoroughly incorporated.

Transfer the mixture to the prepared dish, pressing the dough into an even, compact layer. Bake for 35 minutes. Remove the pan from the oven and place it on a wire rack to cool completely. Grasping the edges of the parchment, remove the pecan bars from the pan. Cut into bars.

Walnut Date Bars

Makes 16

Turn these bars into a decadent dessert by cutting them larger and serving them topped with a scoop of ice cream and drizzled with Caramel Sauce (see page 25).

FOR THE BARS
½ cup water
½ cup orange or apple juice
1⅔ cups chopped pitted dates (about
    10 ounces, with pits)
½ cup chopped raisins
½ cup chopped walnuts
1½ teaspoons pure vanilla extract
1⅓ cups unbleached all-purpose flour
¾ cup packed brown sugar
1 teaspoon ground cinnamon
½ teaspoon baking soda

½ teaspoon salt
½ cup (1 stick) unsalted butter,
    softened to room temperature and
    cut into pieces

FOR THE TOPPING
⅓ cup unbleached all-purpose flour
¼ cup packed brown sugar
¼ teaspoon ground cinnamon
⅛ teaspoon salt
3 tablespoons chilled unsalted butter,
    cut into pieces

PREPARE THE BARS

Position a rack in the center of the oven and preheat the oven to 350°F. Grease a 9" baking pan and line it with parchment paper, leaving about 1" of paper overhanging the two long sides.

In a medium saucepan, bring the water and juice to a simmer. Add the dates and raisins and cook, stirring occasionally, for 8 to 10 minutes, or until the fruit is very soft and thick and most of the liquid has been absorbed. Remove the saucepan from the heat, stir in the walnuts and vanilla, and cool to room temperature.

Meanwhile, in a large bowl, whisk the flour, sugar, cinnamon, baking soda, and salt to blend. Using your hands, rub the butter into the flour mixture until it resembles moist crumbs.

Press the dough evenly over the bottom of the prepared pan. Evenly spread the date mixture over the dough and set aside.

PREPARE THE TOPPING

In a small bowl, combine the flour, sugar, cinnamon, and salt. Using your fingertips, work the butter into the flour mixture until it resembles moist crumbs. Sprinkle the topping over the date mixture.

Bake for 45 to 55 minutes, or until the topping is golden and the edges of the bars are brown and slightly pulling away from the edges of the pan. Remove the pan from the oven and place it on a wire rack to cool completely. Grasping the edges of the parchment, remove the bars from the pan. Cut into bars.

DIRECTORY OF SOURCES

These days, with the Web at our fingertips, there are a thousand and one places to go to stock your kitchen cabinets. Whether you are looking for just the right size pan or a specific kind of nut, online resources can be found that will point you toward what you need. Listed here are a few favorites that I use regularly and consider exemplary, both for the quality of the ingredients and the values of the companies themselves. I also included some additional sources for chocolate, dairy, and flour ingredients.

BROADWAY PANHANDLER

This is a cook's supply store in New York City with a very knowledgeable staff and a great selection of bakeware, cake-decorating supplies, and other kitchenware.

65 East Eighth Street
New York, NY 10003
866-COOKWARE (866.266.5927)
www.broadwaypanhandler.com

EQUAL EXCHANGE

In business for more than 20 years, Equal Exchange is the oldest and largest for-profit Fair Trade company in the United States. They make a very high-quality Very Dark Chocolate bar that is wonderful for baking (and nibbling!), as well as unsweetened cocoa.

50 United Drive
West Bridgewater, MA 02379
774.776.7400
www.equalexchange.com

J&D FINE FOODS

This is a good source for nuts in bulk and the best place I've found to get Brazil nuts inexpensively, aside from picking them out of mixed-nut tins.

4201 First Avenue
Brooklyn, NY 11232
718.768.4790
www.jdfinefoods.com

KALUSTYAN'S

Here's the go-to source for exotic spices and other hard-to-find ingredients such as orange flower water.

123 Lexington Avenue
New York, NY 10016
800.352.3451
212.685.3451
www.kalustyans.com

KING ARTHUR FLOUR BAKER'S CATALOGUE

The Baker's Catalogue is a very thorough resource for bakers, both in terms of ingredients (King Arthur flour, nuts, and nut pastes) and equipment (appliances, bakeware, cake stencils, and other gadgets). King Arthur Flour is also available in many grocery stores. A 5-pound sack of their unbleached all-purpose flour is a must-have for all home-bakers' pantries.

135 Route 5 South
Norwich, VT 05055
800.827.6836
www.bakerscatalogue.com

NEW YORK CAKE SUPPLIES

The mecca for cake making in New York City—with an online store for people not in the New York area—New York Cake carries a huge assortment of bakeware; decorating supplies such as icing flowers, sprinkles, and cake stencils; and by far the largest selection of cake toppers and cupcake papers I have ever seen in one place. Their inventory ranges from the highly professional to the utterly whimsical.

56 West Twenty-Second Street
New York, NY 10010
800.942.2539
212.675.2253
www.nycake.com

ORGANIC VALLEY FAMILY OF FARMS

Organic Valley is a cooperative of farms based in Wisconsin that began with just a few farmers in 1998 and now has 750 family farm members producing organic milk, eggs, and butter, all of which we use when we bake. They also produce cheese, orange juice, meat, produce, and soy beverages. Their products are available nationally in many large and small markets.

One Organic Way
LaFarge, WI 54639
888.444.MILK (888.444.6455)
www.organicvalley.coop

SCHARFFEN BERGER CHOCOLATE MAKER

Based in Berkeley, California, Scharffen Berger makes chocolate both for tasting and for baking. For the home baker, they make a 9.7-ounce semisweet and a bittersweet bar, scored for easy measuring into 2-ounce segments.

914 Heinz Avenue
Berkeley, CA 94710
800.930.4528
510.981.4050
www.scharffenberger.com

SUR LA TABLE

This is a reliably well-stocked catalog with cooking tools and other equipment for home bakers as well as some premium ingredients such as chocolate and cocoa. Retail stores are located across the United States; check their Web site for the location closest to you.

Seattle Design Center
5701 Sixth Avenue South, Suite 486
Seattle, WA 98108
800.243.0852
www.surlatable.com

WILTON INDUSTRIES

These are makers of every imaginable size and shape of cake pan, a variety of cake-decorating tools, and other cake-making supplies. Their products are available through their Web site and at kitchenware and restaurant supply stores.

2240 West Seventy-Fifth Street
Woodridge, IL 60517
800.794.5866
630.963.1818
www.wilton.com

PHOTO CREDITS

INDEX

Boldfaced references indicate photographs.

Conversion Chart

These equivalents have been slightly rounded to make measuring easier.

Volume Measurements

U.S.	Imperial	Metric
¼ tsp	–	1 ml
½ tsp	–	2 ml
1 tsp	–	5 ml
1 Tbsp	–	15 ml
2 Tbsp (1 oz)	1 fl oz	30 ml
¼ cup (2 oz)	2 fl oz	60 ml
⅓ cup (3 oz)	3 fl oz	80 ml
½ cup (4 oz)	4 fl oz	120 ml
⅔ cup (5 oz)	5 fl oz	160 ml
¾ cup (6 oz)	6 fl oz	180 ml
1 cup (8 oz)	8 fl oz	240 ml

Weight Measurements

U.S.	Metric
1 oz	30 g
2 oz	60 g
4 oz (¼ lb)	115 g
5 oz (⅓ lb)	145 g
6 oz	170 g
7 oz	200 g
8 oz (½ lb)	230 g
10 oz	285 g
12 oz (¾ lb)	340 g
14 oz	400 g
16 oz (1 lb)	455 g
2.2 lb	1 kg

Length Measurements

U.S.	Metric
¼"	0.6 cm
½"	1.25 cm
1"	2.5 cm
2"	5 cm
4"	11 cm
6"	15 cm
8"	20 cm
10"	25 cm
12" (1')	30 cm

Pan Sizes

U.S.	Metric
8" cake pan	20 × 4 cm sandwich or cake tin
9" cake pan	23 × 3.5 cm sandwich or cake tin
11" × 7" baking pan	28 × 18 cm baking tin
13" × 9" baking pan	32.5 × 23 cm baking tin
15" × 10" baking pan	38 × 25.5 cm baking tin (Swiss roll tin)
1½ qt baking dish	1.5 liter baking dish
2 qt baking dish	2 liter baking dish
2 qt rectangular baking dish	30 × 19 cm baking dish
9" pie plate	22 × 4 or 23 × 4 cm pie plate
7" or 8" springform pan	18 or 20 cm springform or loose-bottom cake tin
9" × 5" loaf pan	23 × 13 cm or 2 lb narrow loaf tin or pâté tin

Temperatures

Fahrenheit	Centigrade	Gas
140°	60°	–
160°	70°	–
180°	80°	–
225°	105°	¼
250°	120°	½
275°	135°	1
300°	150°	2
325°	160°	3
350°	180°	4
375°	190°	5
400°	200°	6
425°	220°	7
450°	230°	8
475°	245°	9
500°	260°	–

For more information about the Greyston Bakery and the Greyston Foundation's programs, or to make a donation to the Greyston Foundation, please use the contact information below.

GREYSTON BAKERY INC.
104 Alexander Street
Yonkers, NY 10701
www.greystonbakery.com
Toll Free: 800-BUY-CAKE
Phone: 914-375-1510
Fax: 914-375-1514
info@greystonbakery.com

GREYSTON FOUNDATION
Development Department
Human Resources
Real Estate Development and
    Affordable Housing
Greyston Foundation
21 Park Avenue
Yonkers, NY 10703
www.greyston.org
Phone: 914-376-3900

Child Care Center
68 Warburton Avenue
Yonkers, NY 10701
Phone: 914-376-7200

Community Gardens Program
8 Wells Avenue
Yonkers, NY 10701
Phone: 914-375-9002

Family Child Care Training Program
72 Warburton Avenue
Yonkers, NY 10701
Phone: 914-376-7200

Greyston Bakery
104 Alexander Street
Yonkers, NY 10701
www.greystonbakery.com
Phone: 914-375-1510

Maitri Adult Day Health Care Program
23 Park Avenue
Yonkers, NY 10703
Phone: 914-376-3903
health@greyston.org

Technology Education Center and
    Youth Services
64 Warburton Avenue
Yonkers, NY 10701
Phone: 914-376-3610